Chrissy Gruninger

NO FEAR

following the inner
compass of my heart

Also by
Chrissy Gruninger

Rich Coast Experiences Collection

Vicarious Adventures on the Rich Coast

No Fear

Lost and Found in the Land of Mañana

Living Well Collection

A Wildhearted Sanguine Life

An Intentional Life

An Interconnected Life

A Harmonious Life

Nourishing Wisdom

Living Intentionally

Daily Yoga

Table of Contents

Gratitude

Much thanks to those who have supported and encouraged me in the last year.

Mike...thank you for being you. Our friendship means the world to me, and we will always stay connected, no matter how far the distance is between us.

To Lia and Claudio, for your love and support, for making me smile when I didn't feel good and for showing me it is possible to move out of the country and live a fulfilling life.

Amy, thank you for believing in me and encouraging me to follow my dreams. I cannot wait to have you visit me.

Miriam, I'm so grateful to have your peaceful, supportive friendship in my life.

Arlette, I have so appreciated our friendship these last few years; thank you for your presence in my life.

To the team at Cayuga, my heartfelt gratitude for each of you for your support, kindness and generosity.

Thank you to Tammy, for your friendship and kindness.

So much gratitude for Chas and Angie...without you two, I would not have had the courage or strength to try out surfing, much less actually stand on the board and surf.

Silvia, Mau and Nati...thanks to each of you for being my friend and continuing the story with me.

Nicole, I'm so grateful we had the opportunity to meet and share our stories. You will always have a place to stay whenever you decide to return.

My surrogate family from the Cuba trip...thank you.

Ersel, mi amigo, you embody the true spirit of 'pura vida'; your support and friendliness has kept my spirits up and reminded me that anything is possible.

All of you have given me so much this past year in the way of encouraging me and believing in me. I could not have succeeded without you.

Muchisimas gratitud y amor.

"Fearlessness may be a gift but perhaps the more precious thing is the courage acquired through endeavor, courage that comes from cultivating the habit of refusing to let fear dictate one's actions, courage that could be described as 'grace under pressure' – grace which is renewed repeatedly in the face of harsh, unremitting pressure."

Aung San Suu Kyi

Authors Note

After a series of losses and successes, one right after another, I decided it was appropriate to write a sequel to my travel memoir, making it the second book in a trilogy of my adventures in Costa Rica and in life.

The first book was about my travel stories along the Rich Coast. Though No Fear contains some information about traveling in Costa Rica, Nicaragua and Cuba, it is really more about making the decision to move to Costa Rica, and the courage and strength it took to get there. For me, this book is about letting go of all fear and apprehension, which was holding me back.

It's my leap forward into the unknown.

My hope is that it inspires and motivates you, to reach for your own dreams and make them come true. At the risk of sounding like an after school special, my deepest desire is that you understand that no matter how dark the world can be at times, there is always hope and with determination and supportive people by your side, anything is possible. Fortunately, as you can see from my long list of people I am grateful for, I have both.

In the iBooks version, I've compiled photographs to accompany the story. Our planet needs more people, all people really, to speak up for it and protect it, sharing its beauty and wonder. Throughout the book, there are a few poignant discussions and I hope you'll learn something new or at least think about life, and the choices you make, in a different way.

My writing is what I like to call "creative nonfiction". Most everything is true; it may have just been tweaked a little. Some people's names have been changed; both to protect the innocent and to not give credit to the guilty.

While my books are set in story format, my accounts of the places I have visited are all true and I've done my best to give the most accurate accounts. I hope you'll be inspired to follow in my footsteps, experiencing some of the same things and creating your own memories along the way.

The only part that gets a little fuzzy is what I learned in Cuba. This isn't because I've changed the facts but because I'm not really sure what the truth is. There seems to be many different stories and I've relayed the ones which seemed most accurate.

Though these days I am paid to visit many of these places, I will still always give my unbiased opinion. Fortunately, I almost always have experiences that exceed my expectations and I'm so excited to share them with you.

Wellness & Happiness...Chrissy

Chapter 1
Broken Dreams

"I'm glad we had the times together just to laugh and sing a song, seems like we just got started and then before you know it, the times we had together were gone."
Dr. Seuss

We packed up the cooler, secured the kayak on the bed of Troy's truck and headed south for Cambria, one of my favorite little towns in all of California. It was an unseasonably warm autumn day and we had decided to play hooky from work, taking a mid-week getaway to visit the Central Coast.

We took the scenic route, stopping for lunch at Nepenthe and coasted our way down the winding oceanfront roads of Highway 1. Troy had been living with me in California for almost six months now and this was just another perfect day in our blissful relationship. Getaways were commonplace for us; there was so much I wanted to share and experience with him in my beautiful state of California.

San Simeon State Beach was the ideal place for kayaking; very few waves and at that time of year, very few people. It was like we had the entire beach and Pacific Ocean to ourselves.

We carried the kayak out to the shore and I got in the front while Troy waited for the perfect wave to get us over the incoming surf and into the open, calm water. We headed out towards the end of the cliffs where we spotted kelp, hoping to see a few sea otters. We weren't disappointed; two of them were cozying up next to each other. They didn't seem to be afraid of us. Maybe they knew we were in love and wanting to spend a day together at sea, just as they were.

We lazily kayaked around the bay, talking about our travels together and life the last few years. We talked about when we met, in Nosara, and I giggled as we reminisced about our first kiss.

After a little time on the water, we spotted a small private cove. It was hidden, turned away from the beach so the few people on shore didn't even know it was there. We pulled the kayak onto the sandy beach, laid out our beach blanket and took out the cooler. We had packed a few beers, hummus, crackers, and cut up veggies.

After lunch, we curled up on the blanket together for a siesta under the warm autumn sun. Troy took my face in his hands, tilting it towards him and leaned in for a kiss. He whispered in my ear, *te amo.*

It couldn't have been a more perfect day. I was so safe and secure in Troy's arms. He took my hand into his and I rested my head on his chest as we drifted off to sleep.

When I woke up, Troy wasn't beside me. He had never had the chance to come to California. He was gone. I found out several months after his death that he didn't just step in front of an oncoming bus but actually pushed a little girl out of the way.

Here I was again, waking up from a beautiful dream, returning to bleak reality. Some days I wondered if any of the bliss I had felt had been real. It felt like such a very long time ago and impossibly sweet in the midst of the bitter.

***

Coming home from that heartbreaking trip where I lost my love, I turned on my phone as the plane landed. I didn't really expect any messages but I had one text... from Ethan. It said: "I'll meet you in baggage claim."

Ethan lived in Avila Beach, near San Luis Obispo. I couldn't believe he'd driven all the way up to the bay area to be with me. I had known him for almost fifteen years and though there were a few times when Ethan and I thought we might take it further, timing was never on our side. I was relieved that he was there for me, the thought of being alone in my apartment felt overwhelming after experiencing such loss.

As I came down the escalator at SFO, I could see him waiting and I fell into his arms, sobbing. He held me tight and told me all would be okay. It was impossible to believe in that moment but I appreciated the effort to soothe me, nonetheless.

Ethan stayed with me for the weekend. When I'd start to cry, he'd put his arms around me, holding me tight. He cooked me dinner and brought me my favorite soy ice cream. He unpacked my bags, did my laundry, took care of Harmony, my cat, and tried his best to make me laugh, telling me how much he wanted to see me smile. His strength, his being there for me, was just what I needed.

He had to leave early Monday morning but said he'd return at the end of the week. I told him it wasn't necessary, that I would be okay. But on Thursday night there was a knock on my door, and there he was, with our favorite Thai food - pineapple fried rice and pad thai - and treats for Harmony (from the pet store, not the Thai restaurant).

This was how the next few weeks went. We started to alternate places, him coming to see me and then me going to see him. We went hiking, checked out the latest cultural exhibits in the city, and went to the mountains to play in the snow. I took him to Jimtown, my favorite sandwich shop, and to Lake Sonoma for a picnic at the vista point. Little by little, I was starting to feel normal again.

And then, one day, totally unexpectedly, Ethan kissed me. We were just standing in his hallway talking (of all the random places) and he took my hand in his as he pulled me closer to him. It was everything a first kiss should be complete with little butterflies fluttering in my stomach. It was as if a once upside down world had righted itself; it felt so natural.

Later that night, we opened a bottle of wine and went out to his patio. We were having an early Spring heat wave and the night was pleasantly warm. He grabbed my feet, put them on his lap and gave me a foot massage. We talked late into the night... with Ethan, there was always good conversation. We had known each other for so long that we were way past awkward moments of silence and we could talk about anything with each other.

There was such an ease with Ethan that, looking back, I'm not surprised we ended up together. Our timing was still imperfect, having just lost Troy, but I didn't want to miss out on this opportunity 15 years in the making. I was willing to take a leap and let my guard down.

Everything just felt so perfect.

Walking on the beach one morning, Ethan took my hand in his and paused for a moment. He shared with me that he had always felt like I was the one he was going to spend the rest of his life with. He said he believed we were meant to be together, soul mates.

Being the non-committal type, you would think that would make me run in the opposite direction but something about Ethan allowed me to relax, letting me be open to his words and open my heart to the possibility of a real commitment, something I had avoided for over a decade. Ethan and I shared something so much deeper than I had ever experienced, even with Troy.

We had a long term, committed friendship and had always been there for each other. Supporting each other through breakups and divorces (his) had bonded us in a way that we hadn't exactly planned but with Ethan I had a level of comfort which I hadn't really experienced with anyone else.

We shared a blissful Spring season together. The most memorable part was our weekend in Monterey. We went wine tasting, hiking, listened to live music and ended up at a late night diner, of all places, for a very late night meal. I wouldn't normally frequent such a restaurant but when the taxi dropped us off at our hotel, we noticed it was just down the street and being a little tipsy and hungry, we decided to indulge ourselves.

When we weren't together, I was keeping myself busy. Shortly after returning home from the last trip, I had been contacted by Hans, the co-owner of

Cayuga Sustainable Hospitality, and offered a part time job to help them with their online marketing development. I was ecstatic. It was an awesome opportunity. Hans told me he had read my first book and really enjoyed it. He thought I'd be a good match for their team. The best perk of the job? I could visit the hotels during the green season in order to gather new content to photograph and write about.

With this new position, I was able to create more financial security in my life as well as maintain a connection to the country I so loved. While I was still hoping to move there someday, I hadn't yet figured out how I was going to make that happen. This incredible opportunity definitely brought me one step closer to reaching my goal.

It was only a few days into the position that I started planning the next two trips for the 2011 green season. Ethan was happy for me, even though it meant I had to work a few hours each weekend we were together. It was a busy work season for him as well and while he wouldn't be able to go on the May trip with me, he told me he wanted to go on the next.

A few weeks before I left on the trip, Ethan started to withdraw. He told me he was slammed at work and wouldn't be able to visit as often as he'd like. When I said I'd drive down, he told me he'd be working on the weekends and it wouldn't be worth it. Not worth it? That didn't match up with his earlier words about soul mates and the rest of our lives. After all, we'd still have evenings together and I could work on my marketing projects during the day or go out to the beach for a photo session. At that point, I knew something was off but I remembered how Ethan had been there when I really needed him and let it slide. If he needed a little space, I could certainly give that to him.

I decided I'd make my famous chocolate chip cookies and drive down the Friday before I left for the first green season visit, to see Ethan one last time. When I knocked on the door, a woman answered. Someone I had never met before. I asked her if Ethan was around but she told me he was out picking up dinner for the two of them and should be home shortly.

She asked me who I was and when I told her my name, she said, "Oh, the girl who lives up North. It's so nice that Ethan has been able to help you during this difficult time in your life." The only thing I could think of was, "Who is this woman and why is she in Ethan's house?" I couldn't bring myself to speak at that moment. I didn't want to understand what was happening.

I was still standing at the door, speechless, holding the darn bag of cookies, when Ethan's truck pulled up into the driveway. My memory of everything that happened from that moment on is a bit hazy; like it was in slow motion. I turned my head and saw the look on his face. It's one I'll never forget.

I ran down the driveway, passing Ethan on the way. He reached for my hand but I shrugged it off. Now at my car, I was fumbling for my keys -they always got lost in my backpack- when Ethan came up to me.

He told me he didn't know what to say. He said he'd been seeing this woman for a few weeks and wasn't sure where it was going but she lived nearby and he just couldn't do the long distance relationship with me. Plus, he said, he didn't want to get remarried.

I stood there and stared at him. This was all so out of left field. We had never talked about it but I would have moved in an instant had he suggested that the distance was a problem. I probably could have convinced my employer to let me telecommute. As for marriage, I didn't even know if I want to get married. It would be nice to have a partner to share my life with but after all I had been through, I wasn't even sure I was the marrying type. Ethan continued to talk but I had stopped listening.

My body was frozen in place as my mind reeled. "What is wrong with you? If you don't want to be with someone, be an adult and tell the person. Don't cheat, don't lie, don't ignore the person, don't act like an immature fifteen year old kid. You're almost forty-five, for goodness sake."

My emotions were fluctuating between anger and sadness and I was still unable to give voice to the thoughts, fearing that I'd start to scream at him in the middle of the street. I wanted to yell at him, "This was your idea, you're the one who pursued me. You're the one who said you wanted to be with me, that we were always supposed to be together. You had me watch An Affair to Remember because it reminded you of us and Shrek because it defined what true love was, which you said we had."

I reminded myself to breathe. Maybe this was all just another dream?

A really, really bad dream. I mean, wasn't it just a few months ago that Ethan was holding my hand, walking with me on the beach and telling me he believed I was the girl he was supposed to spend his life with? That he loved me with all his heart and couldn't imagine being with anyone else? That he had known it all along but just could never act on it and was so happy we were both now in a position to be together? Unfortunately, this wasn't a dream.

I never spoke with Ethan again. I got in my car while he was in mid-sentence and drove off. I was done.

Unfortunately, I had a three hour drive back home and I cried the entire time. Driving eighty miles an hour in the dark while crying may not have been the safest decision but somehow the universe guided me home and I arrived to a dark house. I didn't bother to turn on any lights or even change my clothes. I just got in my bed and cried myself to sleep. I was devastated beyond words...A fifteen year friendship and potential life long relationship thrown in the trash because of an immature man's failure to communicate.

I just didn't get it. How was I thirty-six years old and still falling for men who lie and cheat? I thought I had gotten all of that out of my system in my early twenties. I thought I had finally found a man who would treat me with respect, kindness and love. It was just the opposite and once again, I was alone, heartbroken and had just lost one of my best friends.

I began to wonder if it was even possible to find lasting happiness.

It was time for a change; I just wasn't sure how I was going to make it all happen.

Chapter 2
The Search for Happiness

"Be who you are and say what you feel, because those who mind don't matter and those who matter don't mind. Dr. Seuss"
Dr. Seuss

I was determined to let everything go. I resolved to move to Costa Rica by early 2012 and make a fresh start. So in addition to everything else I was working on, I needed to focus on how I was going to get my place of employment to allow me to move out of the country and still work for them. I didn't really see any difference in me working from home in Sonoma County (which I had been doing for a few years) and working from home in Costa Rica. My job was totally paperless and I rarely needed to attend meetings. Even if I did, I could still attend a meeting, just via video conferencing.

I wrote a letter to my organization, explaining my need to move to Costa Rica and detailed the logistics, trying to hit on every possible question they could ask so there wouldn't be any delay in responding back with an affirmative answer. I turned the letter in to my supervisor and hoped they would understand how important this was to me.

I wanted to stay with them for the long-term but needed to make some life changes in order to do so. It wasn't just that I wanted to start anew and live in paradise. I did actually have valid reasons for moving. Financially, I hadn't been given a raise in almost four years and they had actually reduced my salary by $15K at one point. Living in California was expensive and I just couldn't maintain my household expenses anymore.

Secondly, my physical health was constantly under attack in Sonoma County. Daily, I suffered from severe allergies but was told by my immunologist that I wasn't actually allergic to anything...I was allergic to everything. Since I wasn't allergic to any one specific thing, there were no medications or treatments that would help me. In Costa Rica, I didn't have any allergies. To put it simply, I felt sick every single day in California and my only reprieve was my visits to Costa Rica.

While I lived in a beautiful area, I was not able to actually experience and enjoy it fully. My health did improve somewhat when I visited the Central Coast (where Ethan lived) but I knew that period of my life was behind me. No amount of lessened allergies could make me sign up for treatment like that again.

The bottom line was that living in Northern California, I felt like I had a cold every day. My body and mind were tired and overall, I just couldn't take it anymore. I had to move. I was too young to be shut in my house and not able to do anything fun or meet new people because I always had a congested head and a tissue in hand. Ethan had been okay with that but he had known me for years. I cringed at the thought of going on a date with someone new and having to blow my nose every few minutes. The dry weather also provided me with severely chapped, cracked and bleeding lips. None of these things made my list of sexy ways to make a first impression.

Though my heart and mind were set on moving, I knew it would not be a quick process to get everything in order. It was difficult to maintain a sense of peace and wellness when I woke up each morning feeling like I had the flu. At times I felt disheartened and while this lifted some as I began

14

planning a life in Costa Rica, I could hardly spend all of my waking hours doing so.

I was faced with a choice. Did I want to find happiness or more discontent? I certainly had enough check marks in my minus column. I could rightfully complain about my heartbreak and health but it would only serve to keep me stuck emotionally, mentally and physically.

I knew that if I want to be an integral part of the world and make a positive difference, I had to do what I could to put aside how miserable I felt. I wanted my life to have meaning and to be of service to others: alleviating the burden that someone else may have through my words and actions.

In an effort to reinvigorate my downtrodden spirit, I recommitted to my choice to live simply.

I simply stopped giving energy to concerns about owning a Coach purse or having an iPhone or whatever else was in fashion at the moment. Keeping up with the Jones never mattered much to me but I realized that it was an exceptionally inefficient use of my energy while my body was battling ill health.

All of those things are just superficial fluff with no real meaning behind it and that's before you investigate the sweatshop labor that creates such products.

I also counted my blessings, performed random acts of kindness, and reminded myself that I am never alone in this world. Even when I didn't feel supported by those who I thought should be in my corner, I knew there were others who absolutely had my back. It was a simple matter of perspective, choosing to find the good rather than focus on the not so great and with that sentiment I packed my bags to head back to Costa Rica for my ninth trip.

***

My last trip to Costa Rica felt like a lifetime ago. So much happened on that trip and continued to happen once I returned that I felt more than a little unsettled in my world. Despite the fact that I truly enjoy Costa Rica, I actually felt nervous sitting in San Francisco International, waiting to board the plane. This would be the first time in four years that I would not be seeing Troy.

Despite all of my best efforts to put myself in a better state of mind, I still couldn't make myself enjoy flying coach. Doing so in the mood I was in was like someone throwing salt in a fresh, open wound. Arriving in Atlanta for my layover, I went directly to the SkyClub, paid the $50 and headed for the bar. The drinks, after all, were free and since positive thinking was failing me, I opted to drink.

Ethan had tried to call a few times over the weekend but eventually stopped trying. I was busy getting ready, finishing up last minute requests at the office and of course, dealing with yet another heartbreaking loss. I had no desire to hear his justifications.

I had had quite a few drinks and was feeling a little numb, just wanting to forget everything temporarily. The flight was delayed because of poor weather conditions and I noticed many flights were actually being canceled. *God help me, please do not cancel my flight.* This is why I always take my trips in May because normally, the tropical storm season hadn't yet started on the East Coast and I wouldn't have to worry about flight delays and cancelations on my connections.

They finally boarded about half the plane but then stopped due to reports of lightning on the tarmac, so we were back to waiting again. Part of me was a little relieved knowing I was not in the group of first class passengers as they were in a big metal machine as lightning was striking nearby. I suppose every moment has its silver lining if you look hard enough. Eventually though the storm passed, we all boarded, and the plane took off about two hours behind schedule.

I slept on the plane, or perhaps more accurately passed out. I'd been up since 2:00am and the drinks in the SkyClub had done their job. Arriving in San Jose made everything better, though. In the past, I hadn't liked this airport because it was crowded, dark and made me feel a little claustrophobic.

Thankfully they had recently completed major renovations and getting through immigration, baggage claim and customs was so much easier as a result. Manolo, who I remembered as my bird watching and sustainability tour guide from 2009, was there to pick me up and take me to Finca Rosa Blanca.

I was arriving late but the chef was kind enough to leave me a plate of tapas in my room, which was beautiful (the room, though the tapas were quite tasty as well). I was in "El Cafetal" and one of the reasons I like this Inn so much is because each room is different. Eclectic would be a better word to use really. I took a deep breath and realized I was *home*.

Everything would be okay.

I fell asleep to the sounds of crickets and woke up to the sounds of chirping birds. They start early here, like 5 a.m., but I didn't care. I was so happy to be waking up to sunshine and warmth sin allergies.

Amongst other amenities, the room boasted an extra-large Jacuzzi tub with a large picturesque window overlooking the Central Valley. I longed to take a good long soak in it, but realized that if I did so, I wouldn't have time to sit on the balcony or take pictures on my way down to the lobby so I opted to skip it.

After a quick shower, I put on the Inn-supplied bathrobe, grabbed my cup of coffee and took a few minutes to sit on the balcony and take in the quiet sunrise. There was a large guava tree to the right of the balcony and I watched as a squirrel enjoyed his morning meal on one of the top branches. He was so focused on eating the little round fruits from the tree. I could see the guava was white inside, meaning it wasn't ripe, but I suppose this squirrel didn't care because as soon as he finished one, he'd scurry around the branches, looking for another. It was nice to take a moment to pause and appreciate the natural world. It was the perfect way to begin the trip.

I eventually got dressed and slowly wandered down to the lobby, stopping to take photos of all the pretty trees and plants whose leaves and flowers were basking in the early morning sun. There are two enormous ficus trees on the property and I loved the way the sunlight radiated through the branches. Leo, Finca Rosa Blanca's coffee plantation manager, met me in the lobby to give me a quick tour of the plantation.

After the coffee tour, I met with Teri, one of the owners of Finca Rosa Blanca, for breakfast. I was so excited to see the French Toast still on the menu. While the toast is good, I was mostly looking forward to the three syrups that came with it: maple, raspberry and coconut. The delicious fresh coffee, made from the organic beans in their plantations only a few feet away, was nothing short of divine goodness.

Teri and I learned that we actually grew up in the same community. What a small world. Our server, Alex, was the same server I had in 2009. It was nice to see so many of the same employees still working at the Inn. The hospitality industry, like many other service based industries, struggles with turnover so when I saw the same people working there, years later, I knew the Inn was treating them well and offering them good salaries and benefits.

After breakfast, I had to quickly gather my belongings and leave for the airport. I was headed back to San Jose International to fly on Sansa Airlines to Puerto Jimenez on the Osa Peninsula. Fortunately, I didn't have to go back into the main airport but instead was dropped off at a smaller terminal, just to the right of the main entrance.

In the terminal, I met up with Maria Jose, my supervisor at Cayuga for the work I was doing with them. She was just stopping by to pick up some items I had brought for their nonprofit partner, Equilibrium. Knowing that I'd be moving (even though there was still no solid plan in place), I thought I could give my old, but unused, art supplies to the nonprofit to distribute to the schools they work with.

It was so nice to finally meet Maria Jose. It felt like we had been friends for years even though it had really only been a few months. While I had seen her at the Harmony Hotel when she was a manager there in 2007, this was the first time I actual got to engage her in dialogue.

After she left, I went through security and sat in the little terminal, waiting for the plane to arrive. I was pleased to see the recycling bins, one each for plastic, paper and non-organic trash. I loved Costa Rica's environmental values so much. The majority of people in Costa Rica might not have had an iPad or Smartphone but it definitely seems they have their priorities straight when it comes to caring for their country.

In the air, I started to think about Troy. We had always talked about returning to Lapa Rios someday as it was one of our favorite places. I wished he could have been there with me, making plans to see the incredible wildlife and experience their amazing vegetarian fare (okay, he was a carnivore but a girl can dream). Looking around to clear my head, I took in the three other people on the plane with me. There was one couple and a single man and I wondered which of them, if any, would be going to Lapa Rios. I tried not to envy the couple their time together.

The flight was an easy one; just about an hour long and it was mostly clear so I had great views of the green, verdant mountains to my left and the seemingly infinite Pacific Ocean to my right. While you're not supposed to get out of your seat in these little puddle jumpers, I did hop from the left side to the right, in order to get photos of both. Some rules were just meant to be broken.

Chapter 3
Osa Peninsula

*"If you want to catch beasts you
don't see every day,
You have to go places quite out
of the way,
You have to go places no others
can get to.
You have to get cold and you
have too get wet, too."*
Dr. Seuss

When I arrived in Puerto Jimenez, the Lapa Rios staff greeted me and the couple at the airstrip, offering us fresh coconuts with reusable bamboo straws in them. The fresh coconut water was unparalleled by the products available in stores in the States. I won't even drink the prepackaged version because the taste is vastly different and it just doesn't compare to the real thing.

Lapa Rios Ecolodge is located on the Osa Peninsula, about forty-five minutes from the town of Puerto Jimenez. It's a private reserve of both primary (about 80%) and secondary rainforest (20%). Since I've already given most of the details about this Ecolodge in my first book, I won't repeat them here other than to say this is my favorite area in all of Costa Rica.

It is one of the most pristine, beautiful and preserved spaces in the country. Open space and jungle is seen for miles with just a few ranches and cows dotting the meadows and hillsides.

As we drove I spoke with the couple and learned that the woman was a model from the Ukraine. Both she and her friend lived in New York but they had only met the day before in Jaco. I laughed to myself as I thought of my brief jealousy on the plane.

It turned out she wanted a break from the hectic life of modeling and the guy was on his fifth surfing trip to Costa Rica. They just happened to meet and decide to travel together, with the guy leaving his surfing buddies behind, changing his ticket home and extending his stay. She was a pretty girl, so I can't say I blame him for his spontaneity.

Before leaving the town of Puerto Jimenez, I asked our driver if we could stop at the lagoon where the caimans hung out. I realized that wanting to get up close to caimans is probably not everyone's cup of tea but it was all just part of the job, albeit one that I love. We did a small detour down the road to the lagoon where not only were there caimans but also an egret rookery with baby birds.

There were a few hundred birds in the tree which was only about fifteen feet from the ground and hung over the pond. I'm sure the caimans, of which there were several, hung out there in the hopes of a baby bird falling out of the nest and into the water. Caimans are a smaller reptile, compared to crocodiles, but they're still big and they're still menacing looking. I walked to the edge of the pond and took a few good shots of the intimidating creatures.

There were two things I couldn't wait for in returning to Lapa Rios: sunrise yoga on my deck which overlooked the beautiful Golfo Dulce and the food. The food was just so delicious at Lapa Rios during my last vacation there. In addition to the high quality and delicious creations what made it even more special was that all of the chefs were from the local community and they were all self-taught. Creating 5-star gourmet meals but never having gone to culinary school just blew my mind; I was impressed that they needed no additional motivation than the quest for excellence.

I was also looking forward to meeting new people. Lapa Rios is a magical place, allowing us all to truly

24

understand just how precious our planet is, why we must protect it and most importantly, how.

The other experience I wanted to have while at Lapa Rios was to see squirrel monkeys. This was the only monkey in Costa Rica (they have four types: squirrel, spider, howler and capuchin/white-faced), that I had yet to see. Maria Jose promised me I'd see them, telling me they were all around the property. I remained unconvinced... Troy and I had hardly seen any wildlife during our five nights there in 2009 and this time I was only going to be there for four, but she assured me wildlife was everywhere.

She mentioned there was even a puma spotted at dusk by two different sets of guests staying in Bungalow 14 in the two weeks leading up to my arrival. Since that was also the bungalow I would be staying in, I committed to being on puma patrol every evening before dinner.

Bungalow 14 also brought my thoughts back to Troy again because we had looked at taking that one during our stay but decided against because it was so far down the path from the pool and restaurant. I would later find out there were approximately 207 steps (uphill, mind you) between the bungalow and the restaurant. On the bright side, it was a good, albeit sweaty, workout in the humid heat three to four times a day.

The first afternoon and evening there were quiet. Well, quiet in the sense of not having too much interaction with other guests. Nothing is quiet in nature; someone is always talking. My first wildlife spotting was about halfway down the path to my bungalow: a toucan. I heard it first, hence why I'm always so passionate about being aware of my surroundings and talking softly when out in nature with others.

Continuing down the path, I came across an almendra (almond) tree full of lapas (scarlet macaws). They were perched there, eating their favorite nuts, breaking open the hard outer shell with their beaks and eating the inside.

Dinner that night, and every night, was somewhat of a sensory experience. They didn't use overhead lights in the restaurant, preferring to add light with candles instead. Due to the portion sizes I received, I would recommend ordering half portions … or just accepting the five pounds you will put on.

Thankfully I had those 207 steps to help me burn some of it off.

Another great thing about their food was that none of it goes to waste. If they had leftovers of a certain product, they'd use it in a meal or snack the next day. You may have sweet corn gnocchi one night and cornbread the next day. Anything that couldn't be used was given to either the pigs on the property or the compost, giving it a second life to become fertilizer for new plants.

After dinner, the sounds of the jungle were even more amplified. Tink frogs (they actually make a noise that sounds like "tink"), crickets, even the fluttering of the wings of a gigantic moth hitting my bungalow's screen, trying to get in, were all a part of the natural experience.

I had a difficult time falling asleep that first night. Between the jungle noises and acknowledging my sadness that neither Troy nor Ethan was with me, I just couldn't get to sleep. Troy and I had shared so many beautiful memories together here in Costa Rica and after losing him, and letting myself be open to the possibility of a new love, I had hoped I'd be able to create new memories here with Ethan. I would have loved to have taken Ethan with me on this trip; he loved the outdoors and would have been in such awe of this inspiring place.

I had to keep reminding myself there was nothing I could do about Troy and with Ethan, well, it was his loss.

***

I was woken up at 4:45 by howler monkeys announcing the early sunrise over the Golfo Dulce. Sadly, a gigantic moth (which was about eight inches in length) had died on my patio during the night, its body just a few feet away from the door. I guess it tried too many times to get into my room and eventually his body just couldn't handle the impact anymore.

Sun salutations seemed appropriate given the rising sun and it felt so good to stretch my body in the humid air. While it was early, the sun was already heating up the local environment. After a shower, I slipped on the lodge-supplied bathrobe and went outside on the deck with a cup of coffee. I was glad I had remembered to order it the night before as I knew I'd need a little pick-me-up before attempting the 200+ steps to breakfast.

Sitting outside on the deck, I could feel a sadness resting deep within me. It doesn't happen often but there is sometimes a sense of loneliness that creeps in to my psyche when traveling alone, this trip more so than others. Mornings always seemed to be the hardest, not having Troy to wake up next to, not feeling his arms embrace me, his soft lips on my skin, the warmth of his body next to mine.

It was as if the natural world knew the emptiness I was feeling and attempted to fill that void.

That morning's sunrise was exceptionally stunning. It had rained throughout the night and everything was so "fresh", as Troy would have said. There was a rainbow off in the distance and I took a moment to be mindful of the beauty surrounding me. I felt the warm humid air surround my skin as I closed my eyes to take a few deep breaths.

With my eyes closed, my hearing became much more profound and I heard a gecko chirping in my room, a bird somewhere off in the distance, and then the sound of breaking branches... lots of breaking branches.

I opened my eyes to see squirrel monkeys in the tree to the right of the bungalow. They were moving fast, flying from branch to branch. It was as if they were running their own version of the Lapa Rios Lapathon, an annual jogathon on the Osa Peninsula with proceeds benefitting the local schools and community.

I couldn't help but laugh, thinking Maria Jose had somehow imported these monkeys and I could imagine one of the staff members hiding near the tree and releasing them one by one.

But all joking aside, Lapa Rios is an Ecolodge created in harmony with nature, allowing humans the opportunity to be in contact with our Earth's amazing biodiversity. It was a setting unlike any other and best of all completely real.

I grabbed my camera and ran back out to the deck but the tree was at an odd angle. Not being able to get a good shot, I raced out the front door of the bungalow and up the first flight of steps, not giving a second thought to the fact that I was in my bathrobe and barefoot.

I should have switched to video at that point because I still couldn't get a good shot. It was so early and as always, I refused to use flash on animals (as it's just not nice), so there wasn't enough light. They were moving so fast through the trees but it was still a memorable experience.

It also meant that I could check off the list of wildlife I wanted to see during my stay; which also included wild jaguars, the Bungalow 14 puma, a golden orb spider, more lapas, green and black dart frogs and the fer-de-lance snake. The jaguars were perhaps a stretch but there's no harm in asking.

On the walk back to the bungalow, I became aware of the fact that I was barefoot and the steps had little bits of gravel. I hadn't noticed them in my previous excitement but they did not feel good on my feet. I didn't think about the fact that I was in my bathrobe; it was early and no one was around.

Once I was inside my room again, I noticed there were many dead bugs – though not as many as when Troy and I had stayed there and the thousands of tiny dead gnats were all over the floor. I noticed one large beetle had been flipped on his back, but was still alive, frantically waving its little feet in the air.

I carefully picked it up, using the "glass and laminated card trick", and took him outside, placing him right side up on the ground. He scurried away into the shrubs and I never saw him again. I was happy to have saved a life. I would do the same for two other insects later in the week, a bee and a wasp. Both of those are more terrifying insects for me to deal with but I didn't want to kill them just because they ended up in my room.

I was scheduled to do the medicine walk tour this morning. Since I was always sick in California, I had a habit of seeking out natural ways to help heal myself. My guide, Edwin, was from the Osa Peninsula and knowledgeable about the many trees and plants in the rainforest with healing properties. He also pointed out all kinds of birds, insects and animals.

My favorite was the golden orb spider and I happily catalogued another mark on my mental checklist. He had me touch the web which was incredibly strong and not sticky at all, like other webs I've had the unfortunate displeasure of walking into back home during my days just out of college as a property manager . The female spider was huge and its mate was tiny. I wonder if its mate was aware of its fate...that after she was impregnated, he would be killed.

It seemed to me that this species really knew how to manage their men and population control. Meet a man, get impregnated, allowing the species to continue, and then kill the man. Not such a bad plan. After all my bad luck with men, I was beginning to wonder what good they really were in the world, other than, of course, to continue on with the human race.

We took the main road back to the property and spotted a family of spider monkeys flying through the trees. The trees were so dense with foliage that it was hard to see and even harder to photograph but I was able to spot two moms with babies clinging onto their backs. It was such a sweet sight to see. A driver passing us by also stopped to let us know about a sloth in a tree a few yards away.

After the hike, I was scheduled for the Lapa Rios waterfall luncheon. Normally, this was a romantic luncheon for a couple but Cayuga had asked me to have the experience it so I would be able to write about it in the future.

I hiked down the path to where the luncheon was held but became distracted when I saw a squirrel monkey troop in the trees. They were so full of energy, chasing one another, and sometimes

31

screaming at each other. While I was being very quiet, I swear one of them threw a tree branch at me. He had good aim as it hit me in the head.

Eventually I made my way to a grove of tall trees with a small clearing and a view of one of the many waterfalls on the property.

Ivan was my server and chef for the meal and he prepared for me a delicious watermelon, feta and cucumber salad to start, which was refreshing after the hike. Or it may have been the cold beer that was refreshing but either way, I began to cool off. The main entrée was a portobello risotto accompanied by bread with garlic oil dip. Dessert was a colorful plate of fresh tropical fruit and a small pot of chocolate fondue. Ivan gave me my space and let me enjoy the beauty that surrounded me.

I could see why so many couples recommended this luncheon... it would have been so romantic to share with Troy. The sound of the waterfall, the birds flying overhead, the wind rustling the tree leaves...it was perfect. It also yet another reminder that I was alone. It was proving to be more difficult than I had anticipated, not having Troy with me. Or Ethan. I loved them both and would have wanted to share these experiences with them but it wasn't possible to do with either. I just had to embrace the moment of being there on my own and gaining the courage to go it alone.

In the afternoon I lounged on the hammock at my bungalow. Well, at least, that's how it started, but my work never stops, especially not at Lapa Rios as it seemed like there was always something to photograph.

So while I did start out in the hammock, I was immediately aware of the toucans, howlers and lizards running around and hanging out in the trees. I was also still on puma patrol. The one little green lizard that I saw must have had a mate nearby as he was flexing his muscles and extending out his colorful dewlap while bobbing up and down. The dewlap is a part of the lizard's throat area that expands.

Walking up to dinner, and any meal really, it always took me way longer than it should to trek between the bungalow and the restaurant. So much caught my eye every time. Flowers, dragonflies, birds, frogs... There was so much magic there and I was like a kid in a candy store. Eyes wide open; there was so much to take in.

Several nights on my way to dinner, I noticed an owl butterfly flying around me. It actually met me every night in the same place as I walked up the hill to the restaurant. And even in the pouring rain, I stood there, trying to take its photograph.

At dinner a couple of nights in a row, I noticed a young couple in their early 20's who looked like they were involved in some kind of religious ceremony. They kept to themselves and definitely weren't drawing attention to what they were doing but since I was eating alone both nights, I was people watching and they caught my eye. On the second night, I noticed they went back into the kitchen and brought out their own food.

We both left at about the same time to return to our bungalows and I introduced myself and asked them what kind of ceremony they were doing. Their names were Danny and Gabi, and they told me they were Orthodox Jews and practicing Shabbat the night before. They also explained that during the rest of their stay, they would be preparing their own meals and had brought their own food and even their own kitchen utensils.

I asked them if it was difficult for them to adhere to this way of living, especially when traveling, but they told me no, it was their way of life and what they were used to. Being such a young couple, only in their early 20's, I really respected the commitment they had to their religion. I don't often have the opportunity to meet people who are truly devoted to a certain practice.

***

The next morning, I once again woke early and sat out on the deck, watching the sun rise between the clouds while waiting for the morning coffee delivery. The hotel also offers tea or hot chocolate but while in Costa Rica I was going to enjoy the delicious, fresh and locally grown coffee. I checked to see if the coffee had arrived (as the staff delivering it were so very quiet) and was happy to find it sitting on the shelf outside the bungalow.

I brought it inside and set it down on the small table where the mugs were kept. I sat down in the one of the chairs next to the table and poured myself a cup, adding the milk, then closing my eyes and bringing the mug up to my nose, taking a moment to breathe in the aroma. It was such an ideal way to start the day.

Upon opening my eyes, I looked out across the bungalow floor to see something that I've always wanted to see... just not in my room. My jaw dropped open, my eyes grew large as I slowly put the cup of coffee down on the side table and focused in on what was a large, fuzzy tarantula. In my room. Not outdoors but in my room.

My first thought was, how long has it been in here? I often left the door to the patio open during the day... did that mean it was in my room all night? Oh no. It could have easily gotten under the bed's mosquito netting and been in my bed. I looked at the glass that I had used to safely return the beetle to its outdoor home and realized there was no way this glass was large enough to encompass the tarantula.

After the initial fear and swearing that went beyond just "oh my god", I took a deep breath and realized it wasn't really moving. I guess it's true what they say...they're more afraid of us than we are of them. Coming to this realization, I immediately grabbed my camera and started to photograph it, probably getting more up and close and personal with it than most normal people would do. Being on the Osa Peninsula is like taking a walk on the wild side, you just never know what you're going to find. And trust me, this is one experience I'll never forget.

At one point, I opened the patio door in the hopes it would scurry outside, even standing behind it and making the motions of "shoo shoo" with my hands but it still didn't move more than a few centimeters. After a while, I became bored with it and found a tiny baby gecko hanging out on the mosquito netting of the bed. I then began to photograph him as he was so cute and little. A few minutes went by and I heard the sounds of breaking branches in the tree outside my bungalow. Not wanting to miss out on anything, I ran out the door only to realize seconds later that I had completely forgotten about the tarantula and had literally just run past it. Oh my god, I could have stepped on it.

If Troy had been here, he would have taken care of it. But I have to note here... even though I didn't personally remove it from my room, I was quite proud of myself for sharing space with it without completely losing my mind. It wasn't like I could easily call reception and have them take care of it as there were no phones in the room and no cell reception on the property. I wasn't about to do the hike up the hill before my coffee.

I finished getting ready, keeping a watchful eye on the tarantula at all times, and eventually headed up the hill to the restaurant for breakfast. Obviously, my first stop was the front desk. I pulled out my iPod which had photos of the tarantula on it to show Diego, one of the front desk team members, and Nicole, an intern from Maryland who would be starting at Cornell in the Fall.

Both looked at it and seemed a little horrified but then Diego pulled out the pamphlet on spiders and pointed out to me that it was a smaller tarantula, also known as a wolf spider. That did little to reassure me. As far as I was concerned, it was still a huge furry tarantula. Although after seeing the photos of the larger tarantulas, I was a little disappointed and kind of wished it had been one of the bigger ones as they had such pretty colors.

Either way, I asked Diego to please send someone from housekeeping to remove the spider before I returned and before it ended up laying eggs in my luggage.

I couldn't wait to share this with Maria Jose...I would later tell her that while I was pleased she had brought in the squirrel monkeys for me, the tarantula in my room was going a little overboard. One of Cayuga's primary focuses at their hotels is creating incredible guest experiences so while I was just joking - they didn't import the monkeys or put the spider in my room - it was a funny thought that maybe they had. A few other people told me that they had run across scorpions in their showers. I added scorpions to my mental list.

I later showed photos of the tarantula to friends at home and my friend Miriam sent me a link about the symbolism of this arachnid. It claimed that when these animals show up in your life, transformation and creativity are manifested. I needed both in the moment and was grateful for the Universe sending them my way.

It was such a pretty day that I decided to sit out on the restaurant patio and enjoy the morning sun before my tour. I noticed a family was sitting at a table across from me and the kids had wandered off to look at something. A few moments later, one of the little girls came running back to the table, grabbed her dad's hand and said, "Dad, I saw a hummingbird and the biggest ever grasshopper. Come look."

While I'm really not sure if I want to have kids of my own, I admit they can be fun to watch. There is so little fear in them as they haven't been tainted by the harsh realities of life. They trust their family will always be there to help them, support them and love them.

***

Melvin was my guide for the Osa Trail hike and he told me he had seen over half of the birds in Costa Rica (there are about 850).

While I do like birds and think they're pretty, I was much more interested in mammals...monkeys, sloths, coatis, agoutis, big cats (despite the fact that they are nocturnal and fairly unlikely to be spotted). There would have to be something pretty extraordinary about the bird for it to really grab my attention.

Like the Lapas or Panama's national bird, the Harpy Eagle, which is not only nearing extinction (making it more interesting for me as a conservation photographer), but it's also a gigantic bird. Its body length ranges from 35 to 41 inches and its wingspan is an impressive 6-7 feet. Another little fact...it's so big that its diet consists of two of my favorite mammals: monkeys and sloths.

During the hike, we came up to a tree that had a small hole filled with water. Melvin pointed out the tadpoles swimming around in it. It was so cool. What a unique place to lay your eggs and hatch baby frogs.

> I loved the surprises nature always managed to provide me in my travels.

At the end of the tour, we crossed over a small stream and hiked up the hill towards the bungalows. We came across a howler monkey family but in the mid-day heat, most of them were taking naps. I decided not to go all the way back up the hill and instead stop at my bungalow to shower and change before lunch.

There were three showers in the bungalows at Lapa Rios. Two in the bathroom, one with hot water and one with only cold, both which looked out to the jungle through a large screened window. Then a third shower was located outside on the private patio. I was using the hot shower inside and noticed two toucans sitting in a tree just outside the window.

With sliding wet feet on the smooth wood floor, I ran out of the shower to get my bathrobe and camera and then out the door to try to get the shot. They were in a perfect location, close by and in good light, but by the time I got outside, they had flown to another spot down the hill and the shot was gone. And there I was again, outside in my bathrobe, this time in the middle of the day with shampoo in my dripping wet hair. It's a good thing the hotel had put me in the last bungalow.

That night I attempted to go on the "night walk tour" with Edwin however a torrential downpour started just moments after we had begun the tour and we agreed it was not worth continuing on. While a light rain is not a problem, with heavy rains even the wildlife was taking cover. It was a little disappointing as this would have been the best chance to see the fer-de-lance snake but nature doesn't always work in accordance with the plans of curious humans.

I dried off and went to the restaurant's bar, the Lapapalapa. There I met Mary and Alec, newlyweds on their honeymoon. A really sweet couple, it was fun to talk with them and hear their stories of all they had seen so far on the trip. They also mentioned to me they planned to return, and once they start a family, bring their children to experience the beauty of Lapa Rios.

Like me they found it comforting to know that even if the property is sold, the new owners are required to keep the forests intact and cannot develop further on the land. Lapa Rios is protected in perpetuity and because of that, Alec and Mary's children will indeed have the opportunity to visit here in the future and experience the same things their parents were seeing so many years earlier.

Afterward I met Juan, Lapa Rios's general manager, for dinner. Juan would be leaving in a few months to go on a year-long, round the world honeymoon with his new wife, Cindy. He told me the story of how they met, the ring he had designed for her and his love of photography. After we were done eating, he brought out his laptop and showed me some of the images from his years of working at Lapa Rios and living on the Osa Peninsula.

They were exceptional. It only made me want to move to Costa Rica that much more... so I could have similar wildlife photo opportunities. The crows in the oak trees in my California backyard may intrigue Harmony, my cat, but they were not interesting enough to hold my attention.

***

While I eat almost entirely vegan in California, I eat vegetarian fare when I travel. As such, I think it's important to know where my food comes from and I decided to visit a local, family owned farm while at Lapa Rios.

When I told Juan I would be going to the farm the next day, he demonstrated how to milk a cow, telling me it would be a lot harder than I imagined. Earlier in the day, Diego taught me how to say "milk a cow" in Spanish and also explained the calf gets to share in the milk production (which sadly does not happen here in the States).

So bright and early the next morning, I went to the farm where roosters were running wild, hens were laying eggs and pigs were eating their breakfast out of large troughs in the front yard. The cows' pasture looked like it was a few hundred acres, with only about twenty cows on the property.

The other thing I noticed immediately? I was definitely wearing the wrong shoes. Note to self: Keds open-toed sandals were not appropriate to wear on a farm, especially not when you're in the cow's barn.

To make a long story short, Juan was correct...it's not easy. I only got a few squirts of milk out but I did make a concerted effort; I was mostly worried about hurting the cow. I also felt bad it was taking me so long as I knew her calf was waiting for me to finish so she could have access to the udders.

After I had given up, we took the small amount I had squeezed and put it in a large bin where they were making sour cream. I was shown how they make it: only skimming the top layer off. I attempted to do it, but again, was only successful a few times.

***

After the farm I walked down to the beach, getting lost along the way. I was used to getting lost in Costa Rica so it wasn't a big deal. It seemed like at least once on each prior trip, I'd lost my way. There are very few street signs in Costa Rica and even in the more rural areas, it was easy to turn down the wrong dirt road and end up next to a cow pasture in the middle of nowhere.

Buying a GPS and downloading the Costa Rican maps helped but still wasn't perfect.

I developed the ability to laugh at my situation thanks to driving on unknown, unnamed, and unpaved roads, with a dead GPS unit, in the pouring rain, running low on gas... It's part of the adventure. I have experienced the joy of getting lost and in doing so, I have learned to be open to the wonders that present themselves in some of the darker times of life.

These days I turn up the radio, open the windows and just let the road lead me. Getting lost has allowed me to step out of my comfort zone, meet new people and see new, beautiful places that I would have missed otherwise. Sometimes, getting lost is the best way to just let go and on the way, find out who you truly are.

This time, of course, I was walking and lost but it made me realize how much I missed driving in Costa Rica. Due to being there for business purposes this time around, I took taxis to and from airports and flew around the country on one of their two domestic airlines, Nature Air or Sansa. It was a great way to get around Costa Rica - carbon neutral and so much faster - but I know there are opportunities I missed out on.

I missed stopping in the middle of a road to take a photo of an iguana running across the street or seeing a caballero herding his cattle on a principal road. I was certain that at some point in the future

I would rent a car and see where the road took me, but in the meantime, I had to find other ways to get lost...and find myself again.

This time, getting lost while walking to the beach, I did get to see some things I wouldn't have seen otherwise and I met a few cute Ticos walking with their surfboards. I figured, if nothing else, they must know the way to the beach. There was a huge swell that week and lots of surfers were heading out to the water.

I never did find the beach I was hoping to see but instead went to the beach Troy and I had been to previously. It was a nice beach but a little rocky, so not as great for getting my feet wet and walking along the shoreline. I took a moment to just sit in the sand under an almendra tree, the same place where I had sat two years before. I looked out to the water, and then closed my eyes, picturing Troy there, swimming in the water and building "zen castles" in the sand with small round stones he found at the water's edge. I was reminded of when he climbed the tree and was hovering above me, smiling and laughing.

When I opened my eyes, I heard the squawk of two lapas flying overhead. You'll almost always see them in pairs as they mate for life and if you're really paying attention, you'll almost always hear them first. If you see more than two, often times it will be their children flying with them.

As I walked back to the main road to get picked up by the shuttle, I wondered if I'd ever find a mate for life. Not living in the same country with Troy, I never really knew if what we had was authentic, although it felt real when we were together. And with Ethan, it was real but didn't last. Or, at least, I wanted to believe it was real. I suppose I have my doubts because if it was an authentic love, then the events that transpired should never have happened.

***

Just before the shuttle came to take me back up the hill, a man walked past me with three horses. I could hear the klippity-klop of their hooves even before I saw them. It was such a nice reminder of how simple life can be. The man smiled and waved as he rode past me.

While I was waiting for lunch, I started to hear noises in the trees and noticed a few people had gathered just outside of the restaurant. There in the trees between the restaurant and the pool was a troop of capuchin (white-face) monkeys. It must have been baby season as several were carrying little ones on their backs. They were flying through the trees, coming up from the lower jungle and making their way across the roof of the restaurant to the other side where more jungle could be found.

What's nice about the Osa Peninsula is that there are so few buildings, built in a way to blend with the natural environment so the wildlife has very little, if any, disruption in their normal life - except, of course, for the humans staring at them.

Maria Jose was right...

Everywhere I looked, there was nature displayed beautifully for me to appreciate, assuming I was paying attention.

At the front entrance, I found a few green and black poison dart frogs. On the way to my bungalow, the gigantic blue morpho butterflies and dragonflies delightfully showed me the way. Walking on the dirt road towards the beach, I came across a howler monkey troop and at the beach itself, I saw land crabs scurrying around, making sand art. I knew that if I was lucky I'd see humpback whales and dolphins as I looked out to the sea.

On any given path, I watched where I stepped as leafcutter ants can be found everywhere, sometimes carrying very large leaves and colorful flowers, bigger than the ants themselves, returning to their colony. I saw a beautiful golden orb just outside of Bungalow 10; its web was three dimensional.

I know I heard green parrots but I never saw them because they blend in so well with the lush, tropical foliage. I did however see eagles and hawks. Coatis and agoutis ran around the forest floor and in the trees. And then there was the elusive puma. I never saw it but I know I will someday.

After lunch, I sat back in the chair and admired the scenery surrounding me. It was a beautiful spot, one I could sit in all day if I actually knew how to relax and wasn't there on business. To my right was pure jungle and in front of me, out in the distance, was blue-green water, where the Golfo Dulce and Pacific Ocean meet. I decided to finish the meal with one of their famous brownies and a cup of coffee.

Later that day, I went on the sustainability tour with Dottie and Lauren, a mother and daughter who were staying at Lapa Rios. For me the best part of the tour was learning how they had changed the living space for the pigs.

When I was there in 2009, the pigs were each in a concrete pen and I felt really bad for them as they couldn't go outside and wander around in the lush green foliage just outside the "barn". The pigs at Lapa Rios are used to produce methane gas in the staff kitchen, which from an eco-standpoint, is a great project as it pertains to sustainability.

It's even better now, since they have installed an electric fence in a large area just outside of the indoor "barn" and the pigs can go out there and live their lives in the fresh, open air.

Still, I have to add that I wish the pigs could just live out their natural lives at the Ecolodge and not be slaughtered for consumption once they got too big. While they don't slaughter the pigs for use in the hotel restaurant, they do sell the meat to local people at a fraction of the cost of what they would normally pay at the store.

It's a nice gesture to help out the local community but still, not enough for this animal activist. Since I wrote in my last book I wished they had more space to roam, maybe by writing my wish that they wouldn't be slaughtered, I'll be able to convince the hotel to become a domesticated farm shelter and allow the animals to continue to produce the methane gas but also live out their natural lives in peace, without fear of slaughter *(hint, hint.)*

I did get another win in the way of animal activism when Lauren decided to question her own ethics about eating pork, after seeing the sweet little piglets interacting with each other. She even made the comment she may never eat bacon again.

This is why I believe it's so important to see where food comes from as it provides a totally different perspective.

It is my fervent hope that when more people see farm animals living, breathing, playing and loving life that they will reduce their meat consumption (if not give it up entirely, like me) or at least insist upon free range, grass fed livestock as it is much healthier for both the animals and the human who consumes them.

Before we had left on the tour, I ran into Hans at the front desk. While we had communicated through email over the last few months, this was the first time I had met him in person. He asked me to join him for dinner so, like the pigs, we could socialize and I could learn more about Cayuga and their properties. We met for tapas and drinks and began our discussions. While waiting for our dinner, a man at a table nearby proposed to his girlfriend. It was one of the sweetest moments of the trip, especially when he said to her, "Just like the lapas, we will be together forever". The entire restaurant was full and everyone clapped and cheered as he put the ring on her finger.

The meeting with Hans went well and it only reinforced my desire to move to Costa Rica and continue my work with his company.

***

With the exception of the cold, everything in Dr. Seuss's quote at the beginning of this chapter happened. After four incredible days and nights where I was in the middle of nowhere, getting drenched in the tropical rain, and fortunate to encounter all types of wildlife from golden orbs and tarantulas, poison dart frogs, caimans, sloths, toucans and scarlet macaws as well as all four species of monkeys found in Costa Rica, I have decided the Osa Peninsula is just like Disneyland...the happiest place on Earth, only a little more wild.

Probably the only downside to Lapa Rios is the rooms only have one single electrical outlet. This was difficult for me since I had two cameras, my laptop, phone and an iPod. I had to get creative in order to keep everything charged. This really wasn't so much a problem as it was an opportunity to accept that I was in a place that encouraged everyone to completely disconnect from the technological world we live in, day in and day out, and reconnect with people and the natural world. That's an idea I can definitely get behind; it was just a little hard to adjust to when I had to get my camera battery charged.

I was fortunate to experience very little rain on this visit to Lapa Rios. It only rained a few nights and sometimes a few warm sprinkles during the day that would always clear to blue skies and sunshine after an hour or so. And just like Troy always said, the rain leaves everything so fresh feeling. I can't say that enough as it's so very true.

As I packed up my bags, getting ready to return to civilization, I wondered...couldn't I just live here permanently, in Bungalow 14? Every day, breathing in the fresh air, getting morning coffee delivered, being greeted by wild animals, enjoying an afternoon thunderstorm while laying in the hammock under the bungalow's eave...wouldn't that be nice?

Chapter 4
Manuel Antonio

"We are all travelers in the wilderness of this world, and the best we can find in our travels is an honest friend."
Robert Louis Stevenson

After leaving the primary jungle, I flew to Quepos, to stay at Arenas del Mar Beachfront & Rainforest Resort which is located in Manuel Antonio. We were flying over Ballena National Park at low tide which meant we could see the "whale tail" out of the plane windows. It was an awesome sight to see from above as the natural reef along the Uvita coastline really does look a whale's tail.

Arriving first in San Jose, I then had to check back in for my flight to Quepos and I learned there was an earlier flight, leaving just fifteen minutes later. I paid the $15 and called the hotel to advise them of my early arrival.

The only problem I experienced is when I went through "security" (in quotes because it's not like normal airport security) and the agent checking my toiletries told me I could not bring my baby powder on the plane. It was in the travel size Johnson & Johnson packaging that couldn't even be opened without breaking it apart and I was shocked that they would think it be dangerous in any way. It's not as if baby powder could possibly be confused for cocaine.

I ran back to the counter agent to try to get my bags so I could put it in the checked luggage but it had already left for the plane. After a little pouting, the agent agreed to let me get the luggage from the plane and put it in there for the flight.

At the Quepos airport, the driver that picked me up had the air conditioning blasting. In my travels with Troy, I learned that a/c really isn't necessary and he told me most locals don't really like it. They use it because it's what they think tourists want. So I knew when I asked if he would mind turning off the a/c and just open the windows he would be happy to oblige.

Arriving at the road to the hotel, I was shocked to see it had been paved since my last visit. Hallelujah. It was an infinitely more pleasant experience...and safer too.

The thing I wanted to do the most while there was sit on the lounge chair of my balcony at night and listen to the waves below me while looking up to see the billions of stars in the dark night sky. I only had a few days at Arenas del Mar but my itinerary was crammed with adventure and new, cultural learning experiences: hiking in Manuel Antonio National Park, going on a spice tour at Villa Vanilla, learning how to make tortillas and taking a tour of the property to better understand the sustainability programs the hotel offers.

I checked in at the front desk with Marvin, who I remembered from my visit there in 2009, and noticed a white face monkey hanging out in the ceiling rafters. I wondered why there hadn't been animals around like that when I was there two years before.

In 2009, while I had heard the howlers, I never actually saw any monkeys on the property.

I was beginning to wonder if I was just lost in love at the time, being

with Troy and not noticing anything else happening around me.

I met with Maria Jose and Jorge for an early lunch at Playitas, the Resort's beachfront restaurant. Jorge, or George as he's often called, works at Cayuga as their Operations Director.

It was so nice to finally meet all these people who I'd been communicating with for the last few months. Another thing I noticed was how they always greeted me, and others, with a hug and a kiss on the cheek. That was so different from my experience with coworkers in the States where we barely acknowledged each other at the office and during business meetings. Sometimes even friends and family members greeted each other less affectionately than my Costa Rican associates.

After we finished our meal, I took a golf cart up the hill to my room. I was going to take full advantage of having a golf cart available to me after four days at Lapa Rios where I was hiking up those 207 steps, a few times a day.

The room was lovely, with a huge bathroom and large closets. It had a separate sitting area and large bedroom along with three sets of sliding glass doors that opened to a private patio with two sets of lounge chairs, a separate sitting area and a hot tub. I turned off the air conditioner and opened each of the doors in order to hear the waves crashing on the beach below and let the fresh air in.

Surprisingly, I was actually a little overwhelmed when I finally got settled into the room. Arenas del Mar is a new Resort which opened in 2007 and unlike Lapa Rios with its one outlet, there were at least twenty-two outlets in the room that I could find, ten outlets outside on the balcony and two dataports in the room. There was also a phone in the bedroom and the bathroom which you could use to make free international calls. The sitting area had a minibar stocked with free Costa Rican snacks and coffee from Finca Rosa Blanca. It was the total other end of the spectrum from where I had just been.

It had been raining on and off all day so I took a moment to sit on one of the patio chairs with my laptop, using the free wifi offered by the hotel and enjoyed the sound of the rain falling just a few feet away from me.

Once it stopped, I ventured out to the lobby where I ran into Ersel, one of the guides and my main contact for blogs and other online content at Arenas del Mar. Just like Maria Jose and Jorge, he greeted me with a warm smile, a hug and a kiss. He was about to take a family on the tortilla making tour and asked me if I'd like to join them. The idea of freshly made tortillas made my mouth water. How could I refuse?

We walked down to the employee area and met Carmen, the house mom, if you will. She was all set up for us and Ersel translated as she demonstrated how to make the tortillas. Then we each had a chance to make our own. I have to admit that none of ours came out as perfect as Carmen's but it was really fun trying. It was especially fun to watch the kids as they tried to make their tortillas with the help of their parents. We then enjoyed the tortillas, adding a little sour cream on top along with a cup of coffee made in the traditional way using a chorreador de café (a small wooden coffee maker that uses a reusable cloth filter).

Returning to the room, I decided to order room service for dinner and call it a night. I did go outside to sit on the balcony but it was overcast and there were no stars to enjoy. The crashing waves became a meditation for me and I sat there quietly for a few hours, letting the warm humid air relax my body and mind.

***

The next day, on the way to the Villa Vanilla Spice Tour, we picked up a woman at another hotel whose husband had decided to go fishing, unsurprising since Quepos was known for its sportfishing and I'm sure that was more exciting to him than a tour of a botanical garden. She was a nice woman, living in New York but originally from India. We were both excited to learn about the spices and visit the garden.

Do you ever wonder what your food looks like as it's growing and before it arrives in your market? Would you recognize black pepper in its original state or a vanilla bean before it's dried and liquefied? Do you know what cinnamon looks like or how it grows? Can you tell the difference between turmeric and ginger? How about chocolate...any idea what that looks like before you purchase it in a bar at the store?

You may ask, why do I need to know what my food looks like when it's growing? I believe the reason is two-fold:

We need to maintain the interconnections we have between our Earth and ourselves and it's important to understand how much time and effort goes into creating the food we so simply purchase at our grocery stores.

I feel we are losing the connection to our food as well as our planet as everything these days is packaged and processed. When I met with Jorge, he made the comment how he thought it was so odd that our products in the States come in boxes. He used cereal, one of the most common staples in the United States, as an example. I never gave it much thought since I grew up on Raisin Bran and Life Cereal. Didn't everyone eat breakfast out of a cardboard box?

I decided to make it my mission to not only understand where our food comes from, what it looks like in the growing stages, and then to share that information with others.

My hope with this next section is that you'll begin to appreciate the food you eat and be excited to share your new knowledge with others too...

To start, did you know vanilla bean comes from an orchid flower? How cool is that? Much of the world's vanilla is now artificially produced due to expense as well as agricultural and weather issues in the regions where it can be grown. Most vanilla cannot self-pollinate in order to produce the flower; therefore it must be pollinated by hand. Because of this, a lot of work goes into the production of a vanilla bean. Once ready, the pods must then be harvested and dried, eventually being turned into the liquid we purchase in the spice aisle of our grocery stores.

Did you know the cinnamon you probably have in your spice rack isn't really cinnamon? It may say it on the label but in the United States, our cinnamon is most often a product called "cassia". True cinnamon is called "Ceylon" and originated in Sri Lanka. Ceylon and cassia are related to one another but offer different characteristics in taste and fragrance.

Cinnamon is a tree whose bark is used to create small pieces of the product. When first sliced, the bark appears white however as it dries, it turns a brownish/reddish color and begins to curl. It is then dried and sold as whole bark, more commonly called "cinnamon sticks" or made into powders.

Black pepper actually starts out as a green seed pod. Turmeric and ginger look alike from the outside, both having a similar color and below-ground root structure, but turmeric has a bright orange color when cut open.

Last but not least, chocolate is produced from the cacao tree and starts off as a tiny little flower hanging off the trunk and branches of its tree. It then grows into a pod which can be a variety of colors: white, green, even pink and magenta.

When harvested, the chocolate beans inside the pod are white. That is not "white chocolate" which actually isn't chocolate at all. White chocolate is artificially made with sugar, milk, vanilla and cocoa butter but no actual cocoa solids. Sometimes, it doesn't even have the cocoa butter in it; vegetable oil is often substituted in cheaper products. So check the label and make sure it at least contains the cocoa butter.

As for real chocolate, the white cacao beans are then dried which, if I understand it correctly, changes their color to a darker, brownish/reddish hue.

Throughout the garden, we saw birds, frogs and even walking sticks, the latter being incredibly difficult to see as they were in a tree and looked like small, thin branches. However when you got up close to them, you could see that they had a tiny little face in the center of their body.

We ended the tour at a ranchito overlooking a beautiful valley. Our guide prepared cinnamon iced tea and vanilla bean cheesecake for us as well as hot cocoa and vanilla ice cream with a ginger cookie, which was probably my most favorite part of the tour.

***

Arenas del Mar offers happy hour at the bar every night and also offers fun, educational events in the main lobby next to the bar. The previous night, Ersel had given an interesting lecture on the sloth. That night, it was to be salsa dancing lessons. While at the bar, I met two women who were traveling with their husbands. They were from Virginia Beach and had just arrived from a few days at Arenal.

When they learned about the work I was doing for Cayuga, they were so excited. I would come to find that every guest I spoke with, when mentioning the work I was doing, would be in awe. They all wanted to know how I got the job, what my background is, and why hadn't I moved down there yet. Many admitted to being a little jealous. I can understand that, I would be too if it wasn't me in this position. Before I went to dinner, I mentioned to them I'd be going on the Manuel Antonio National Park tour the next day and they eagerly agreed to come along.

I also noticed that when I would mention this was my ninth trip, people would give me a certain quizzical look. I guess making nine trips to the same country in five years is a little odd, but I love it here so much. There is always something new to see and do.

The next morning I slept in...until 6 a.m., that is. I had left the sliding glass doors open the night before and there was actually a little sunshine peeking in through the windows. It had been raining on and off for the last few days and I was happy to finally see the sun rising over the hillsides of Manuel Antonio, especially since we were going on a 4-hour tour that morning and rain would have made it a less pleasant experience for the guests who I had talked into going with me. I started the coffeemaker and got ready for the day. I was loving all of the electrical outlets at this point and always getting a full charge on my camera batteries.

After a quick breakfast, I met up with Ersel and our group. It consisted of a young couple as well as the two couples I had met the night before. Ersel was an exceptional tour guide; you could tell he was not only informed about his subject matter but also loved what he did.

On the way to the Park, he talked to us about what we'd be seeing and doing on the tour. I thought it was great that he spoke in Spanish for part of it, using hand gestures to help explain the words he was saying such as monkeys, birds and sloths. While most of the people didn't speak Spanish, they appreciated having the experience of learning a few new words in an easy, non-intimidating way.

Arriving at the Park, my mind drifted to the last time I was there with Troy. We hadn't communicated well that morning and ended up at the beach, instead of going on a hike. I knew that my tour with Ersel would follow a similar path but I was hoping to see more flora and fauna along the way.

I was not disappointed. While Troy would often spot different kinds of wildlife when we went into the country's parks on our own, it was an entirely improved upon experience with a hired guide. The last time I was in Manuel Antonio, we saw no animals on the main path as Troy was focused on getting to the beach. I only came across the white faced monkeys and Jesus Christ lizard when we arrived at the beach and headed off on my own, leaving Troy to "take a sun". This time, Ersel was stopping us every few feet to point out something interesting. I photographed bats on tree trunks, baby green iguanas, baby black iguanas, white faced monkeys, sloths, caterpillars, butterflies, spiders, frogs and grasshoppers.

Ersel asked us to try to find the walking sticks in the shrubs and later provided us with the opportunity to eat termites. Thankfully, my vegetarian ways got me out of the latter without losing face, but several of the other guests did try the termites and said they tasted a little "woodsy".

Just before the beach, we passed by the huge anthill that I remembered from two years before. It had been the first time I had seen anything so massive. The mounds were enormous, with a rich reddish brown dirt and many feet wide as well as high. They often appeared to just be huge piles of dirt but looking for the little holes where the ants came in and out let us know that we'd found a colony.

Arriving at the beach, a few people went into the ocean and I wandered off down the path to see if I could find any monkeys. Sadly, there were no monkeys to be found this time but Ersel told me that was actually a good thing as it meant there was enough food higher up in the forest and the monkeys didn't have to scavenge at the beach.

I came across a huge black iguana, which appeared very old and wise. It was hanging out on a piece of driftwood near the water's edge and let me photograph it until someone got too close and scared it away. I am often frustrated by the lack of respect people have for the wildlife and the fact that they ruined my photos by trying to get up close to it. I wondered if they realized that since they weren't pets, they would flee if approached.

Later we saw another one on the path, eating a small fruit. Ersel told us he was eating the fruit of the Manzanilla tree, which is poisonous to people and most animals, except for the iguanas. In Spanish, the tree is known as Manzanilla de la muerte or "little apple of death". I joked to my companions that perhaps these were the apples the wicked queen was trying to get Snow White to eat.

As we headed out of the park, we came across a coconut stand and a man with a machete. (note: there always has to be at least one man with a machete in each of my books). He offered us free pieces of coconut and a few people purchased one to drink.

My last night there I tried the Bailey's cheesecake. It was so rich and delicious. The perfect way to end a good meal and a great day.

63

Chapter 5
Returning to Harmony

"So long as the memory of certain beloved friends lives in my heart, I shall say that life is good."
Helen Keller

From Quepos, I flew back on Nature Air, arriving in Pavas, near San Jose. My luggage was over the allowed weight and I had a third piece I was using as a carry-on but the man at the counter only charged me $7, which was a lot less than what the actual fees would have been.

I then took a flight from Pavas to Nosara, stopping in Tambor and Punta Islita on the way. There was a young man in front of me on the plane and after we landed in Tambor, we started to chat. I learned he was not only going to Harmony, but doing a summer internship there as well. Brandon was a student at Cornell and like Nicole, had never been to Costa Rica but both thought it would be a good place to acquire hotel management experience.

Our driver picked us up and we took the "short-in-distance but long-in-time" drive to the hotel. The roads in Nosara will probably never be paved and therefore, cars have to drive slowly both because of the bumps, dips and rocks but also because of the dirt that gets kicked up, sometimes making it hard to see if there hasn't been much rain to moisten the road.

As we turned down the road toward the hotel, I felt like my heart stopped for a moment. My chest became tight and a sense of sadness overtook my body, mind and spirit. It was there that I knew I had to say goodbye to Troy. Harmony, after all, is where we first met.

I started to make plans for how and where, but just before checking in, I got distracted as I ran into a famous celebrity staying at the hotel. In order to respect his privacy and not turn myself into a shameless name dropper, I shall let him remain anonymous. I can say that he was an incredibly good looking man though. I had been told the day before that he had checked in and was so excited he was the first person I saw upon arrival.

Even though I was still having a difficult time breathing, now it was from excitement and not sadness. The nice part was that everyone, guests and staff, gave him his privacy. He was traveling alone and just wanting to surf, do yoga and spend time in the community. He even attended the local surf competition that Saturday and was gracious in hanging out and taking photos of himself with the locals.

After that nice little welcome, I checked in at the front desk and was told I'd be in Coco #5, the same room I was given in 2007 when I met Troy. I had mixed emotions about that. Joy, because it was such a sweet memory of our meeting and the nights we spent together but also sadness because it reminded me he was no longer here.

***

During my stay in Nosara, one of the activities I had slated for myself was surfing. On my first day there, I met the girl who runs one of the local surf shops, Angie, but I didn't feel like I was quite ready to get on a board in the ocean. Fearing the open water, I instead decided to try stand up paddling in one of the local rivers which was still quite the adventure and fortunately, considering the number of times I fell, the water was warm and refreshing.

When Spencer, the owner of Experience Nosara picked me, Harmony's operations manager and Brandon up for the adventure, I showed him my brand new waterproof camera and he advised me against taking it with me. I told him not to worry, that I was sure it would be okay.

Unfortunately my certainty was overruled the first time I fell off the board and the camera fell out of my board shorts and into the river...never to be found again. A brand new Sony camera, a 16GB chip and many photos and videos that hadn't yet been transferred to my laptop, but none of that mattered. After losing Troy, I realized the saying was true: don't sweat the small stuff. Sure, it was a brand new expensive camera but it was just a camera. I could buy a new one and the photos could be retaken.

Like I told Spencer, all was okay. Plus he can now tell the cautionary tale any time a tour participant shows up and wants to bring their camera with them.

The experience of stand up paddling on the Rio Nosara was amazing. I can be really uncoordinated at times, especially in new situations, and this time was no different. I had horrible balance, continually falling off the board. However, as soon as Spencer mentioned that there were crocodiles in the river, my feet suddenly became affixed, like they were glued, to the board. That was all the motivation that I needed and there was no way I was going to fall off again. At one point, Spencer thought he saw a baby crocodile and all I could think was...where was its mother?

I also had an issue with running into the mangroves. Mangroves are an important part of tropical ecosystems and consist of trees and shrubs with really tall roots that stick out of the water, which are quite painful when you run into them. It's even more embarrassing when you're unable to get out of them, though. Of course, my board just kept taking me directly into them. I know, I know, I needed to learn how to steer and paddle properly. Spencer made it look so easy. My companions also showed me up quite easily as Sofia never fell off her board and Brandon only fell once.

We eventually made our way out to a beautiful black sand beach with tons of driftwood (*read my first book to learn more about my obsession with driftwood*). We could only stay a few minutes though as Spencer could see the storm clouds forming and he wanted to get us back to the car before it started to rain.

Even with all of the mishaps I experienced, I'd still do it again. Once I got the hang of it, it actually became rather meditative and I could picture myself doing this sport more regularly, on my own, as a contemplative practice.

A few months later, I saw an article online about people doing yoga while on a stand up paddleboard. Seriously? I had a hard enough time just standing on the board and these people were doing full backbends and headstands.

The next day I met with Gerardo, Harmony's sustainability coordinator, and learned more about the sustainability projects Harmony offered and what they were doing to give back to the local community.

Harmony Hotel's concept is one of simplicity, yet subtle luxury at the same time. It's located only steps from the beach, with high eco-standards, friendly staff and absurdly good food. Especially given its location which is pretty much in the middle of nowhere.

Harmony is also known for being a mecca for surfers and yogis and as such, their restaurant and Juice Bar offers delicious, healthy and sustainable meals. Adjacent to where you'll find the good food is their lovely Healing Centre and Spa...to restore those tired muscles after a day on the water or in the yoga studio.

I didn't get to partake in any yoga classes or spa treatments but I did thoroughly enjoy the meal I shared with Gerardo on my last afternoon there. The sandwich was full of flavor, made with goat cheese, tomatoes, salsa, greens and honey on freshly baked multi-grain bread. I also highly recommend their cookies for dessert. The chocolate chunk and almond cookie is my favorite.

I enjoyed talking with Gerardo and was happy when he joined me for dinner that night as well. We share a lot of the same philosophies and it was fun to learn about his travels to the States and hear about his perspectives and experiences. He told me when he was in his teens, he traveled to Orange County, California and one of the things he noticed was that every shrub and tree was perfectly maintained and manicured. That definitely matched my experience of Orange County as well, though not just the plants but the people too. It reminded me of how grateful I was that I no longer lived there.

While I was at Harmony for three nights, it went by so quickly and I couldn't believe how fast Monday came. I had to return to San Jose and I took my last walk on the beach that morning before breakfast. As I walked barefoot along the short path to the beach, I could hear and see little Halloween crabs scurrying around, taking cover, fearful of what I might do to them, although all I wanted was their photo. There was one though, hanging on a branch eating its breakfast (a leaf) that let me take its photo that morning.

As I continued to walk, I was surrounded by lush green plant life along with the sounds of birds flying overhead and the waves crashing in front of me. There was no one else at the beach at that time and it was so quiet and peaceful. I knew this was the right time to say goodbye to Troy.

On our first trip together in Tamarindo, Troy had walked out to the beach and collected a pretty shell for me. While I normally leave shells at the beach, the gesture was sweet and I accepted it with a smile. I had brought the shell with me on this trip and with it being the last day in Nosara, I walked out to the shallow water and cast the shell back into the ocean, saying goodbye to Troy at the same time. I needed to let go and returning the shell to the sea, where it belonged, seemed like the appropriate way to do so.

***

Upon returning to San Jose, I met up with Michelle, founder of the nonprofit Earth Equilibrium with whom I had been volunteering for a few months. She is also Hans' sister-in-law and so after our meeting, we drove to Hans' home to join his family for a lovely dinner. Maria Jose was also invited.

Hans' wife, Jennifer, had prepared a delicious meal of raclette, which is kind of like a fondue meal. When I first informed Hans and Jennifer that I was a vegetarian it threw them a little, especially when I told him I didn't eat fish. However the meal they prepared was perfect. We enjoyed great conversation in both Spanish and English. After two weeks, my Spanish had improved (slightly) and I actually could understand much of what was said.

The following day, I attended the Cayuga corporate meeting at their office which is just a few blocks down the road from the hotel. Maria Jose had given me directions, telling me to go up a few blocks, turn right and then walk down a few blocks. (Remember, there are no addresses in Costa Rica.)

Well, that wasn't totally accurate and I ended up going around in circles, having to ask for directions a few times. The other problem was there were two or three buildings, all with the same name, within a few blocks of one another so I wasn't sure which building was the correct one. Fortunately, everyone I asked was very helpful and I eventually found my way to the correct office. When I arrived, Maria Jose had realized the directions were wrong and apologized for the mistake, but like I said before, I didn't mind getting lost; it was just a part of the journey.

For lunch, we all went to a Chinese restaurant and I was beyond disappointed to see shark fin soup on the menu. It's such a horrible practice to kill the sharks for their fins, generally discarding the shark back into the water after they cut the fin, letting it suffer as it slowly dies. I hope someday this practice will be banned worldwide as sharks are a vital part of our planet's health and it's estimated that we've already eliminated over 90% of them from our oceans.

The meeting continued after lunch but after two weeks of traveling, my body was starting to feel rundown and I decided to return to the hotel to take a siesta before meeting up with Silvia for dinner. Silvia had become a friend over the years and is the owner of into-designs.com. I was hoping to also see Mau, one of her design assistants, but she told me she had school that evening and wouldn't be able to join us.

We had dinner at a delicious Asian restaurant in San Jose, Tin Jo, which not only offered a large vegetarian selection but their food was sourced from sustainable locations as well.

Being able to create these global connections with people, culture and food allows me to better understand and appreciate the oneness and beauty in our world.

After twelve airport transfers and eight flights in fourteen days, I returned home exhausted but also so very radiant (not just from my tan but my spirit as well). Costa Rica is full of richness, culture, good food, friendly people and an abundance of incredible wildlife and plant life not to mention remarkable landscapes and vistas. I feel so fortunate to have had the opportunity to travel there during the last five years, meet so many good, kind people and to be able to share my experiences with others.

Central America was truly where my heart felt the most free and where I felt healthy, alive and vibrant. I knew there would come a time when I would call Costa Rica Home. For the time being, however, I left my heart and spirit behind and returned to the sterile beauty of Northern California.

Chapter 6

Inconveniences (+ a few short tangents)

"I still need more healthy rest in order to work at my best. My health is the main capital I have and I want to administer it intelligently"
Ernest Hemingway

By day 2 of my return home, the beauty had faded. I ran errands for a few hours outdoors and for the next four days, I was severely ill, barely being able to get out of bed. It wasn't a cold, it wasn't the flu. It was just my daily life having returned back to Northern California.

I had to find a way to permanently move to Costa Rica...Where I could step outside or sleep with the windows open and not worry about waking up in the middle of the night with allergies.

If it weren't for the bugs, bats, snakes and enormous spiders in Costa Rica, I would sleep outside on a hammock. My eyes don't water nonstop there, my nose doesn't run, my ears don't ache and my body actually feels healthy. My head is clear and I'm so much more productive when my head isn't congested and hurting all day long.

Fortunately, I worked from home, so the symptoms were not as severe as they would be if I actually had to leave my house every day but I missed having the freedom to do so. Imagine the Seinfeld episode about the "boy in the bubble" and that was how I felt.

I knew I wouldn't sleep well but I powered through the day and went to bed early every night, sometimes before the sun had even set because of the overwhelming fatigue. If the fatigue didn't knock me out, the three antihistamines I took every night were sure to do the trick. On the bright side, antihistamines were also given as a medication for people with anxiety so this little bonus probably helped me maintain, to a certain degree, my sanity while being trapped indoors.

Until I could move, I knew I had to find peace, every day, in Northern California. As best I could, I tried to overlook the pain my head and body experienced and stay motivated to make a difference... both in my life and the lives of others.

I refused to go through life in neutral or in a perpetual state of negativity.

Finding peace meant accepting my current circumstances and trying to do my best every day to create more peace, love and joy in our beautiful world.

At odds with my desire to create peace though was my irritation with family and friends who did not support me. Many, including members of my family, just could not understand my life choices. Mind you, my parents are really good and kind people but it had been over a year since I spoke with my family and the last conversation I had with my mom in 2010, I was asking her, once again, for the money they had set aside for my wedding so I could move to Costa Rica.

You see, in my mind, moving to a new country was *my* major life event. Just like opening a new business, adopting or having children or getting a divorce.

I told her I was not going to have a wedding and therefore would appreciate their support with this other major life event. My mom, not understanding, said to me, *"Chrissy, you're still so young, you'll find someone to marry"*. Oh...bless her heart.

I didn't say I would never get married, I just said if I did, I would not have a wedding, at least not in the traditional sense. I have tried to explain this to them multiple times.

My thoughts on weddings are that they are incredibly wasteful and destructive to our natural environment. People fly from all over the place to watch two people tie the knot. A frivolous amount of money is spent on flowers (which usually have pesticides), dresses (probably made in sweatshops), jewelry (which more often than not has someone's blood on it), food (often dead and not organically grown), and wedding registries...don't even get me started on those.

Nowadays, with people getting married later in life, they are just replacing what they already own so it's creating more waste. Given that fifty percent of marriages end in divorce, why would I want my parents to spend all that money on one single day? The wedding money could help start me off on the right foot in my new and unknown life ahead rather than choosing to blow it all on a single day. To me, that sounds pretty responsible.

The differences in opinion didn't start and end with weddings. My family really didn't understand my life choices across the board. I failed to see how being a world traveler and choosing to live abroad, while admittedly less conventional than settling down and starting a family with a white picket fence and all that comes with it, could possibly be any less brag-worthy.

Besides, I'd managed a few conventional accolades as well. I owned two homes, completed graduate school, owned my own business and wrote several books. I'd never used drugs and never been in jail. I didn't have a drinking problem (although drinking myself into oblivion was beginning to look better and better between the heartbreak and the allergies) and I've accomplished a lot more in my life than others who are my same age.

For some reason, none of that ever felt like it was good enough. I knew that my parents didn't owe it to me to support me financially in any way but at the same time I couldn't help but wish that they'd invest a little in my dreams for my future instead of their visions for me.

***

If you can't walk the walk, don't talk the talk.

To add to that growing frustration, the nonprofit where I worked was one of those that could never make a decision in a timely manner. It was two long months before I finally heard back from them that they weren't going to let me move out of the country. Not to worry though, I had already moved onto Plan B. Given my recurring health issues, I wasn't going to let anyone stand in my way at this point.

One of the reasons provided for declination of my proposal to work from Costa Rica was because it was a "third world country". The organization claimed that they believed in, and actually had an entire program devoted to, expanding people's worldview and consciousness. When they labeled Costa Rica a third world country, I was horribly appalled (and it just put fuel on the fire motivating me to leave this job as soon as possible).

The term third world country is offensive and I encourage everyone to stop using that term. First of all, we all live on the same planet, so there can't be three worlds as there are not three Earths. Second, if you're going to use a term to describe a less developed country then it would be a "developing country". Thirdly, I also believe you should understand what it means for a country to be "developed" or "developing" before you employ such terminology at all.

While I didn't expect everyone to understand my take on global economics and development terminology, I was horribly disappointed that an organization that professed to maintain similar values to my own had been so thoughtless. Two of their major programs had to do with holistic health and healing and creating a more global worldview.

I saw their decision as hypocritical and short sighted, however the final straw came several months later when they advised me I had to come into the office one to two days each week. I, in turn, mentioned not only my sensitivity to being outside of my home but also advised them I had broken my tailbone (I'll get to that story shortly) and couldn't sit at a desk without being in pain.

The response from executive level management included a suggestion to go on pain management (AKA potentially addicting drugs) for my tailbone in order to be able to come into the office. I won't even get in to all of the ways that suggestion was out of alignment with their holistic health objectives.

Since at the time of writing this, I'd made ten trips to Costa Rica in five years, I feel like sharing a few comparisons to back up my perspective:

According to my Environmental Science 101 textbook (which also does not use the term "third world"), "Costa Rica, with an average per capita income of only $8,860 (U.S.) per year, but a high level of democracy and stability, is in the high human development category." The Human Development Index is a UN based program which evaluates "real quality of life". Costa Rica is also #1 on the Happy Planet Index and the US is a dismal #114. Now, given those stats, where would you rather live?

I'm not trying to say Costa Rica doesn't have any problems; I'm just trying to improve people's perspective and hopefully create a more expansive worldview, and not just about Costa Rica, but our world in general.

People say Costa Rica is poor or "third world" because of things they see: such as bars on the windows, homes that aren't in excellent condition or that there isn't a mall in each town or a Starbucks on every street corner. Or maybe they haven't even been there but they may hear about it from friends or make assumptions based on what they hear about Latin America in general.

This may not be very popular to say but I invite people in the US who think this way to come down from their ivory towers and go visit one of our inner cities or rural areas, here in the States.

There are bars and plywood in windows, lack of books, desks and supplies in our schools as well as dilapidated infrastructures, multiple families living in small apartments, poor nutrition, obesity, lack of health insurance, homelessness (over ½ million people), hunger, guns, prostitution, domestic violence, child abuse, gangs, drugs, crime, murders...Sounds pretty "undeveloped" to me.

As for malls, coffee shops and other common US services, maybe we need to ask ourselves if all that stuff is really important. Is all of this "stuff" making us happy and improving our quality of life?

Many people have a warped perspective because they only choose to see what they want to see and they ignore what they don't want to see. I had someone once tell me he felt the average "middle class" citizen in the US made over $150,000. If that were true, my income would be at, or below, the poverty level. Of course, as he said that, he was sitting in his dining room in his 3,000+ square foot home in Bel Air where a huge original Arvid hung on the wall above his head.

I invite you to think about what truly makes up your "quality of life" and to open your mind, expanding your worldview to new opportunities, cultures and experiences. If you don't know about another country, don't just make assumptions based on what you see or hear. Talk to people who live there, do your research and learn about the country before you pass judgment.

Chapter 7
Plan B

"To accomplish great things, we must not only act, but also dream; not only plan, but also believe."
Anatole France

It has been said that you can live on a "hope and a prayer" but after the denial from my job, I was feeling the need to look for something a bit more tangible.

While I may value open-mindedness and spontaneity while traveling, I was not the type of person who could just make a major life change out of the blue. I knew that I needed a plan. Since receiving financial assistance or emotional support from my family was more or less out of the question, I needed to come up with real, practical ideas in order to get myself down to the Rich Coast permanently.

My body always felt tired and rundown from the allergies which only served to make my mind and heart feel just as tired. When I saw an ad for a special at a local gym, I figured if I could make my body stronger, maybe my mind, heart and spirit would follow. I decided to hire a personal trainer, Chas, and started working out daily, sometimes even twice a day.

At the same time, I signed up for Spanish classes and put my focus on that which would get me down to Costa Rica: doing what I love, photojournalism, and using my experience working with nonprofits to help Equilibrium.

So my plan then, leading up to the move, was going to be focused on putting myself first. I needed to relearn how to be strong and to follow my dreams, even when those who I thought should be supportive of my goals actually thought I was making a really big mistake. I was listening to my instincts and I knew I was doing what was right for me. I had done that in the past and it worked out pretty well.

In 2005, I decided to sell my home in Aliso Viejo, California, a city near Laguna Beach. Just like now with the move to Costa Rica, I really wasn't supported by most of the people in my life when I made the decision to move to Northern California. And while I really had no knowledge of real estate market trends, I just knew in my heart it was the right time to sell. People pleaded with me to hold on to it, telling me I'd never be able to buy another home in California and the prices would only continue to go up.

Well, as well all now know, I made the right choice. Home prices in the community where I sold are now back down to the price I paid in 2002 and much, much less than what I sold it for in 2005.

Sometimes when instinct pipes in with its two cents it's hard to listen, either because of fear or because others try to tell us it's the wrong thing to do. Yet when I choose to listen to my heart and act on the advice in a mindful way, I am always presented with great opportunities. I didn't just up and sell my house in 2005.

I actually began thinking about it, and what I wanted to do with my life going forward, in the summer of 2004. It was in Spring 2005, after much thoughtful consideration, that I made the decision and felt the timing was right.

That decision to move has been such a blessing for me over the last several years. It has opened up new doors and opportunities that I never would have had in Orange County. I can't say life has been totally perfect...no one's is. Mistakes have been made along the way but I also know those mistakes have taught me lessons and have reminded me to be more present in my everyday life.

Nearly seven years later my heart, once again, was telling me that it was time. While I'd always thought of myself as a true California girl, after my first trip to Costa Rica in 2006, everything I once believed about myself changed.

I think, if we are truly connected to our divine self, we each have a place where we're meant to be, at any given time.

I knew my decision to move from Southern California to Northern California seven years earlier was the right one. I didn't have any regrets and had learned so much from my experiences about myself, others and the world around me.

I sometimes felt like Northern California should be its own state; it is remarkable how different it is from Southern California. There was very little pollution, less traffic and people smiled at one another, acknowledging each other's existence. There was actually "open space", just acres upon acres of hillsides and meadows. Friends who visited from Southern California were always in awe, each one remarking on the difference.

While I had enjoyed my life in California, it was time to move on to the place where my heart truly belonged. When I first conceived of the goal in 2008, I had no idea how I was going to do it. I needed to have money in the bank, the ability to work and continue to make money to support myself and I needed to find the right place to live. I was determined to make this move happen.

And fortunately, the more I focused on this goal and allowed myself to be open to the idea, the more the puzzle pieces started to fall into place and I knew I'd be living in Costa Rica soon.

Chapter 8
Finding My Breath

"All you need is the plan, the road map, and the courage to press on to your destination."
Earl Nightingale

For the next six months, I met with Chas before sunrise, three mornings a week. I really couldn't have asked for a better personal trainer. I knew it was early for him but I worked for a restrictive organization. Though they allowed their employees to work at home, which sounded progressive when they first allowed it, they were very much tied to the old old-fashioned notion of requiring their employees to be chained to their desk from 7 a.m. – 5 p.m., Monday – Thursday.

For example, I was once told that even though I worked from home, I wasn't allowed to do a load of laundry during my lunch break. Given that philosophy, I guess I shouldn't have fed my cat during the day either. I've always disliked working for companies that micromanage their employees that way. I know that I will meet my deadlines and work best for employers that choose to trust me in that regard.

In the beginning of the personal training, given that it was so early in the morning, I felt a little responsible for providing fun entertainment to Chas. I would talk a lot about my travels, the tarantula, baby monkeys and other fun stories.

At one point he told me one of the things he would remember most about this point in his life was how early he was waking up to meet with me. He smiled when he said it so I don't really think he minded too much.

He also thought I had the coolest goal: to learn how to surf. Since I had just taken the baby step with standup paddling in June, I was determined to get on a surfboard when I returned to Harmony in November. While Chas had never been surfing, he came prepared to every session, having researched what it would take to get me to have the courage and strength to stand up on a surfboard and ride a wave. What an awesome summer it turned out to be. Most days, there was very little fog and lots of sunshine.

That was what was keeping me sane – warmth, sunshine and my early morning workouts. I finally felt like a little bit of light was shining into my spirit again. Even though I still couldn't go out and enjoy it because of incessant allergies, my home was warmer and brighter and every little bit counted when I was stuck indoors.

Even with all of the great things happening in my life, my heart felt empty. As much as I tried to work it out of my body, I couldn't get the negative energy out of my heart. As the summer months came and went, my confidence also began to wane about when, or worse, if I'd be moving to Costa Rica in 2012. And this only increased the emptiness in my heart.

What made things even harder was the show I always felt I had to put on. People were always telling me how my life was so great and how jealous they were of me.

If they only knew the half of it. They only saw the half I wanted them to see. I know, for the most part, I've had a pretty good life. I was raised in an affluent community, I received a good education and was given many opportunities most kids in the world only dream about. I was grateful for all that life had given to me but at the same time, it was as if I had a little dark cloud that followed me around - kind of like Pig-Pen in the Charlie Brown series.

Thanks to my perpetual tap dancing (figurative), I was the only one who saw that dark cloud. Not that others didn't know about my some of my struggles but they'd always tell me how resilient I was and comment on how I always bounced back from whatever negativity was thrown at me.

The fact was, I was tired of always bouncing back. I was pretty tired in general, to be honest.

Working multiple jobs and having to maintain a household at the same time was getting to be too much. Something had to give. I was tired of working full time and not having anyone else who could help me with the daily household responsibilities. I was tired of the daily struggle with my health; I just wanted things to get easier.

I would beg the universe. There were days when I just wished the world would crumble before me and I wouldn't have to deal with any of it anymore. Feeling sick and rundown every day was not good for my health, physical or mental.

Expenses were starting to pile up as well, especially with all the medical issues I was facing. Add to that my single income household and really, any way you look at it, it is way harder compared to a two-income family. Unless of course the two-income family isn't able to manage their money or has an unexpected life change like a divorce. Even then, there's still the likelihood of alimony and ongoing assistance.

It's challenging and tiring to be responsible for everything. As a single person household, I had no one to turn to for support. Even if I'd asked for help, none would come. I was on my own. And really, unless you've been in that situation – *of being on your own, being responsible for everything, with no other means of support, financial or emotional* - you really can't understand. And that was something I had to accept of the people who told me No when I asked for help. It's also why it just became easier not to say anything at all.

Still, I had to deal with all the effects of my emotional and physical fatigue.

One night, I forgot to lock my door and in the middle of the night, the wind blew it open. It wasn't until 6 a.m. as I came down my stairs, that I noticed. Immediately panic set in.

First I had to find Harmony (who thankfully was sleeping in his bed) and then I ran around the house to make sure nothing was taken. I lived in a relatively secure neighborhood but one can never be too safe.

There were other instances that reflected the fatigue I was feeling. I would often forget to take my medications or worse, wonder if I had just taken it minutes before because I couldn't remember so I was either not taking it all or doubling the dose.

At one point, I actually considered interviewing strangers to live at my house, rent-free, and in exchange, take care of the house, cooking, cleaning, bill paying, grocery shopping, etc. Pretty much, I wanted and needed a live-in personal assistant.

With all of this going on, I had to continually refocus my energy on what would get me to my goal. At the same time, I had to come to terms with the fact that maybe it wasn't going to happen. If Equilibrium didn't get funded, I couldn't live and work in Costa Rica, at least, not with my current salary at Cayuga. There always seemed to be something holding me back.

Still, I was determined to find the courage to say YES to life. I had just finished writing a book about it and figured that I should probably follow my own advice. I'd found that over the years, so many of us live our lives in a neutral state and we miss out on so many incredible opportunities.

In the past, I would often say things like "When I..., then I..." but living in this neutral state wouldn't allow me to move forward in life or be open to new people, opportunities, and experiences.

I learned that living in that neutral state was often fear based. Fear of being rejected, losing control, or of the unknown. But life is full of unknowns. I couldn't know what the next day would bring; I only knew what was happening in any given moment.

So instead of living with fear and missing out on all of the incredible experiences life had to offer, each day, I had to learn to let go and choose life, even when I was feeling miserable.

Again it came down to my choices. I had to choose to wake up every morning feeling radiant, choose to be healthy, happy and harmonious with every thought, word and action and choose to love my body even though I felt like crap most days.

Those choices made space for me to be able to choose to stand up for what I believe in and to do things now rather than waiting for that "perfect" moment.

From experience, I knew obstacles would always come up and try to get in my way of living a healthy, happy and harmonious life. That is just the way it is. Life is like a rollercoaster ride with ups and downs and unforeseen twists and turns along the way. By saying YES to life, I was releasing myself from being held back, to create new experiences.

I knew I had to trust myself, connect with others and step into the life I deserved. No matter what, I was moving to Costa Rica.

***

I purchased a few lottery tickets but they never won me more than a few dollars. I knew there was no easy way. The only way to make my dreams a reality was with hard work and determination.

Nothing has ever come easily for me in my life so the thought that it could all magically happen with one lottery ticket was a little absurd. Sometimes, you have to try the easy road to be reminded that there is no such thing.

In contrast, my life seems to have taken the road less traveled and while it may not be a clean, paved, straight, easy road, it was still mine. Uneven, rough, unpaved dirt road with winding switchbacks, potholes and rocks were my thing. It's why Costa Rica felt like home.

Of course, metaphorically and physically there also always seemed to be a river to cross, requiring a little extra oomph but I have the spirit of an SUV – without the gas guzzling disregard for the environment.

I had to accept I could no longer live life to the fullest in my current situation.

I was trapped in Northern California, by my sensitivity to the local environment and my dependence upon my job to make enough money to cover the costs of basic necessities like food, clothing and shelter. I had to come to terms with the fact that my life had been put on hold, but at the same time, I also knew it was time to release the pause button.

I came to the realization that not only was it was no longer acceptable to me to work for a company who didn't walk their talk.

I also had to acknowledge it was no longer okay for me to do my part time job, that I loved, on the side. I needed to make my part time job, full time. For years I had been doing side work and I was okay doing both, but now, with everything else going on, I knew I had to make this part time gig my real job, to step out of the shadows and into the light. I had to follow my bliss.

I created budget spreadsheets and started selling off my belongings. I researched the cost of moving and contacted people about rentals in Tamarindo and Nosara to find out what it could cost to live there. I created a checklist of things I was looking for:

A safe neighborhood
A short walking distance to the store would be nice but not absolutely necessary
Near the beach...well, okay, that was a given
Monkeys nearby would be a nice perk

I wanted to live simply and imagined what it would be like to see my life packed up in just a few small boxes and pieces of luggage.

There were still days when sadness would take over but for the most part, I was keeping myself busy and staying focused. The one thing I couldn't bring myself to do was write. Ever since Troy's death, I'd suffered from writer's block. I tried freehand, typing, even just jotting down notes was hard. It was even harder when I tried to sort through the notes and figure out what my shorthand meant. It was so very frustrating, not being able to bring the pen to the paper or my fingers to the keyboard.

I'd sit for hours, just staring into nothingness. Because of my allergies, I wasn't motivated to go out and hike, or photograph, which probably was also contributing to the writer's block and overall lack of creativity. I don't think I was depressed, just sad. Sad for the loss of Troy, then Ethan, and sad that that the goal of moving to Costa Rica seemed so far away.

I'd read about people who let go of everything and just followed their passions, succeeding along the way. My life had never been that way and I really didn't have faith in rainbows and unicorns. Without the family support I'd seen others have, I really only believed in my ability to white knuckle it, but on the plus side, I knew that I wouldn't let myself down.

I was determined to continue moving forward, making relationships with others and being inspired by those around me. If my family didn't understand my choices, that was just fine. I'd just build myself a new family. There were many people who came into my life during this time and were an inspiration. One was the incredibly spirited Rina, a yoga teacher from Miami. It was at a workshop for her new book, Choose Peace, that I had to come to terms with the feelings of emptiness and loss from my relationships and truly acknowledge there was a void.

We met for dinner afterwards and I learned that she was half Cuban. The funny thing was, Cuba kept showing up in my life in the oddest of ways. After dinner, I offered to photograph her book signing event at a bookstore in Mountain View. As it would turn out, the bookstore was on "Castro Street". I had told Rina about my desire to go to Cuba and the signs that kept popping into my life and we both laughed when we saw the street name. I knew, both from within myself and from Rina's book and coaching, I needed to find inner peace.

Relationships, food, alcohol, exercise, even yoga was not going to fill the emptiness in my heart from the losses I had experienced that year.

I settled on yoga because, when done with the right mindset, it would always bring me back... to my breath, to my heart center, to the core of who I am.

Yoga had been a part of my life for almost two decades by this point. As a yoga teacher, I challenged myself to not only practice my yoga on the mat but to also take my yoga practice with me throughout each day, consciously choosing each of my thoughts, words and actions in order to create positive effects on others (and as little negative impact as possible).

Considering all that had happened with Ethan and the loss of Troy, I decided to reassess my relationships through the eyes of yoga. I knew I needed to find a way to maintain a healthy, loving, kind partnership and in general, create more positive, supportive relationships.

Yoga was an excellent place to build stability for my relationships because there were so many similar components: flexibility, balance, strength, commitment, acceptance, patience, humor, courage, mindfulness and practice (to name a few). They also required love, peace and joy; towards oneself and others.

With yoga, I tried to flow into each pose with ease, nurturing my body as I breathed more deeply. Often times, I needed to make an adjustment, opening my heart more, pressing my shoulders back and down, lengthening my spine, reaching forward. Other times, I need to use a block, belt or bolster to provide me with a little extra support. Sometimes I need to give myself a little more space, bending my knees or taking a wider stance.

And yes, sometimes, I stumbled and fell, but then I took a breath, smiled, and returned to the mat, making small adjustments along the way so I could do better the next time.

As I worked through my yoga practice each day, I tried to develop new ways to ease into the more difficult poses with grace. As I did that, I noticed a shift in my body and mind. I knew, in my life off the mat, I needed to allow myself to be open and present to new experiences and recognize that what seemed so difficult at first may not be as hard as I once thought. Life didn't have to be a constant struggle.

With my relationships, I also came to the understanding that they don't always last. I chose to assess and appreciate what each one had brought into my life, what I learned from them and what I wanted moving forward into the future.

My mantra for my daily practice was simple::
breathe deeply...in all moments.

Whether I was attempting Virabhadrasana 3 (Warrior 3) or facing a challenge in one of my relationships or life in general, I knew that strong, grounded breaths would sustain me. Before moving into the pose or engaging in a difficult conversation, I reminded myself to close my eyes and take a deep breath, letting any fear or distress release on the exhale.

This small action of finding my breath made a tremendous difference in my life and my practice. I hadn't been that clearheaded in months. It was no wonder I was struggling so much with writer's block. I had forgotten to breathe.

***

In early October, I decided to follow the signs that kept popping into my daily life, telling me to go to

Cuba. I signed up for the Christmas week tour, booked my flight to Miami and took a deep breath. I didn't really have the money for this trip but all the signs were there that I should go. I had such a strong sense that it would be a meaningful and worthwhile trip. Plus, I just needed to give myself a break. I had an upcoming trip to Nicaragua and Costa Rica at the end of the month, which of course would be another incredible opportunity, but I knew I'd be working the entire time.

With the Cuba trip, while I would be photographing and journaling every moment, it was work I was doing for myself and not for anyone else. I hoped it would be therapeutic to spend some time exploring a new country and learning new things about myself and others.

About a week before I left on the trip to Central America, I had an injury, actually two. First, while training with Chas, I flew off a balance ball and landed on my knee. Chas, who was always very protective, felt so bad about it but it was totally my fault; I just wasn't paying attention.

Then, a week later, only days before I left, I fell down my hardwood stairs and injured my tailbone. I also landed on my right side and there was a huge dark bruise there as well. I can't lie - that was painful. I wondered how was I ever going to manage sitting on a plane for several hours.

Thankfully, I was flying first class which was a bit more comfortable and spacious than the last flight in coach and then there was always the Advil PM and a free glass of wine to knock me out.

Chapter 9
Nicaragua

"People who don't travel cannot have a global view, all they see is what's in front of them. Those people cannot accept new things because all they know is where they live."
Martin Yan

Stepping off the plane and making my way through customs, I was relieved to be officially on vacation from my regular job.

Actually, I had asked my office to let me work fifteen hours during the two weeks I would be traveling in order to stay somewhat caught up but I was told no. However, I was also told that I had to check emails every day in case they needed something.

I was incredibly irritated by their double standard. I had to work if they wanted me to and I couldn't make any major plans during the day in case I was called into work. I felt as though I was still being held hostage by this organization, being told to sit around and wait to see if they needed me to do something. At this point, I had one foot out the door. Even with Equilibrium not yet getting the funding we needed, I was determined to move on.

As I reached the front of the immigration line, I pulled out $5 and handed it to the agent but apparently the fee had doubled since I had been there last. Nicaragua had realized they could charge more to tourists for their entry taxes. $10 was still less than the $28 fee Costa Rica was now charging as a departure tax though.

I picked up my luggage, made my way through customs and stepped outside, taking a moment to appreciate the humid air. It was about an hour drive to Jicaro's boat dock and I decided I'd try to practice Spanish on the way with my taxi driver. Overall, I did okay with small talk and learned a few new words.

103

It was a gorgeous day with blue skies and sunshine and a few white clouds hovering above us. On the boat ride to the Lodge, we could even see the cone shaped Concepción Volcano on Ometepe Island in the distance. Herons, egrets and ospreys could be seen in the treetops, diving into the lake for their afternoon meal.

Considering the fact that Nicaragua and Costa Rica had experienced two weeks of continuous rain, ending only days before I arrived, I was relieved to see the sunshine. As with my previous trip I had a list of requests for the Universe.

Prior to my leaving, I told Maria Jose that I wanted to have blue skies, sunshine and to see turtles hatching. I didn't think it was really that much to ask. I had quite a laugh when Maria Jose wrote me back to say that turtles were more expensive to import than squirrel monkeys but she would try to have baby turtles hatch at the Harmony palm tree when I was there. I also appointed her with the responsibility of preventing rain during my visit.

Normally, when you first arrive at Jicaro, a few of the team members will meet you at the dock and greet you with a cold drink, wet towel and give you a tour of the property. I was happy to see the cold drink and towel but since I had already been there the year before, I didn't need the tour and just wanted to settle in and have a little lunch.

Considering Jicaro is a tiny island (only about one acre), it was amazing how the food was so fresh and diverse. Most everything was sourced locally, either from farmers on the other islands or nearby in Granada. Being vegetarian, my meal options were a little more limited, but always good. In speaking with other guests, I was told that their lunch and dinner options were always delicious, especially the fish, which was caught daily in the lake.

After enjoying the Gallo Pinto "burger", I briefly met with Howard, Jicaro's General Manager, who was leaving on vacation for the week but told me to be sure to relax during my stay and enjoy the Jicaro Experience. I didn't really know how to relax, but I assured him that I would enjoy my time there nonetheless.

I was in Casita #4, the same one I'd had on my first visit. The architecture of the casitas was stunning. While simple in design, you could still tell how much effort went in to creating them. There were so many little details that made all the difference between being a boring hotel room or an architectural creation. I also noticed they had installed a railing on the staircase leading to the second floor. I remembered having a few missteps in the dark during my last visit so the railing was a welcome sight.

Before dinner, I went to the bar as one of my assignments for the week was to taste test the various alcoholic beverages and blog about them. It's a rough job, but somebody's got to do it. Of course, I rarely drink hard alcohol, not since high school really, but it was part of this week's job description. And I rarely drink any alcohol at home but there was something about being in the tropics that welcomed a cold beer. I met a lovely couple while at the bar, Mary and Steve, who were celebrating their 30th wedding anniversary. They were originally from Canada but living in Colorado. Over the next few days, they would invite me to share many meals with them, which was a kind gesture as I so often ate alone on those trips.

The first drink I tried was the Jicaro Sunset. It had very pretty colors of orange, red and yellow and actually matched the sunset we were watching over Mombacho Volcano. It tasted good too; the primary alcohol in it being liquor made from the Jicaro fruit. It also had passion fruit juice, banana and coconut milk.

I learned that Mary and Steve, when living in Canada, had made several trips to Cuba and I was immediately interested in hearing their stories. I found it fascinating to meet people who were not from the States, as the overall impression of Cuba was always one of beauty and friendliness. When I talked about Cuba at home, I often heard opinions based on stereotypes people believed about places they had never visited and was usually met with suspicion and apprehension.

Service at the bar and restaurant was often slow but it wasn't due to staff laziness or an unwillingness to work. It's simply an issue of a culture that functions at a slower pace. Most people in the States are completely unaware of the rushing and don't understand how to slow down and enjoy the moment. I eventually brought myself to a level of comfort with embracing the slothfulness, but it took me a few days. I knew that I had to at least try though,

After all, I was on a private island with only nine casitas, an infinity pool, spa, 360° lookout point, yoga deck and open air restaurant. There wasn't much that could be done in a fast-paced way. O

ne might think you'd get bored here but the total opposite was true. Beyond relaxing, eating and drinking on the island, there are many activities to do off the island. More than I was able to fit into one trip.

The island is about an acre in size and it's said Jicaro's island was formed when nearby Mombacho volcano erupted tens of thousands of years ago, blowing off most of its cone shaped top into Lake Nicaragua below, creating the hundreds of little islands that make up Granada Isletas.

It's also said there are sharks in the water because the river connecting the lake to the Caribbean Sea can, at certain times, get wide enough to allow larger sea life into it. Although Howard assured me the sharks are at the other end of the Lake and are never in the waters surrounding the island. It's the largest lake in Central America and over 3,000 square miles in size. Not to worry, those sharks were way at the other end of the lake.

At dinner that night, we discussed how Mary and Steve learned of Jicaro and why they decided to travel to Nicaragua. While their friends all had concerns about them coming to Nicaragua, they in contrast were excited to visit and learn more about the country. We talked a little about the Sandinistas

107

and the country's past but we mostly talked about what they wanted to learn and experience during their trip and the activities they wanted to do.

I recommended a few of my favorites and things I hadn't done last time but wanted to try. Of course, it was all weather dependent but if the rest of the week was anything like my first day, there wouldn't be any issues. The weather was perfect (*thank you Maria Jose*).

***

Coffee delivery service wasn't until 6:30 a.m. so on my first morning there I decided to take a moment to meditate while the sun rose over the lake. These last few months of getting back into my daily yoga and meditation practice was really making a difference in my overall mental wellbeing.

Being in Nicaragua, of course, improved my outlook on life even more. Anytime I could go someplace and feel healthy, without allergies or the resulting fatigue, was a good thing. The added bonus was being able to wear shorts and a t-shirt at 5:30 a.m. and not be cold - something to be cherished as it would all go back to normal in a few weeks.

I didn't have any tours planned for the morning so I took my time enjoying coffee on the casita's private deck and eventually made my way to breakfast. I ran into Mary and Steve and they asked me if I had heard the rooster at 4:30 a.m. I told them yes, and I remembered that same rooster from a year ago, cock-a-doodle-doodling at the same time. We all laughed and agreed we needed to give the rooster a name. Mary thought Rory was a good name and so Rory the Rooster it was named.

There's nothing you can do about nature, domesticated or wild, and we all understood that; it was just part of the experience. Might as well make the most of it.

I ordered traditional gallo pinto for breakfast, or Huevos Nicaraguenses, as they call it at Jicaro. It's slightly different from Costa Rica's version but the main elements are the same: rice, beans, eggs. A light rain had started to fall but by the end of breakfast, the clouds had once again cleared out to blue skies and sunshine.

Not having anything pressing to attend to, I made myself comfortable on my deck's hammock. Every casita at Jicaro overlooks the lake and lying there, I took a moment to relax, enjoying the sounds of the natural world around me. I could see Great Egrets skimming the surface of the Lake, looking for their next meal and above me in the trees, there were beautiful flowers opening in the sun's light.

Since I can never really relax, every few moments I'd pop up to see something else that was flying by or moving in the trees above me. That's when I started to hear a "plopping" sound in the water below me. I assumed it was a bird finding fish but didn't see any birds in the water below. I kept leaning over the hammock though, looking at the water as I could see ripples being created and knew there must be something down there. Eventually, little heads surfaced for air... turtles. I nearly rolled out of the hammock I was laughing so hard. Maria Jose had done it again. While these were not exactly the turtles I had originally asked for, I was still happy to see them. There's just something so unhurried and methodical about a turtle; a good reminder to slow life down and appreciate the moment.

Around lunchtime, I wandered out to the open air restaurant and had a delicious soup which had a little "kick" to it, accompanied by freshly made bread dipped into their olive oil and banana vinaigrette (one that should definitely be bottled and sold Stateside). Mary and Steve were at another table and we all agreed to go into Granada with Julio, Jicaro's main tour guide, for a tour of the city. While I had already done this tour the previous year, I wanted a refresher and to take a few new photographs.

What I didn't realize was that Julio had something else to do that afternoon and instead I would be adding "tour guide" to my resume. While I was a little apprehensive about taking this couple on a tour around Granada, I was also excited. I have somewhat of a photographic memory, so I remembered the general layout and knew getting around the town and seeing the most common things like the square, churches and outdoor market would be easy enough.

Our taxi dropped us off at the Fort and the driver said he'd pick us up at the cannon near the Square in two hours. The Fort appeared to be closed but with a little coaxing, the security guard let us enter, telling us we could only stay for a few minutes. At least that's what I thought he said as he only spoke Spanish and much too fast for me to pick up all the words.

Despite my photographic memory, I don't have the best recall when it comes to the actual details of historical events, so that was somewhat lacking in the tour I was gave. I simply couldn't remember all of the stories I had been told the year before about the town's history. I did my best, talking about pirates, the Spanish conquest and the ousting of William Walker. I think Mary and Steve were pleased overall with the experience.

We saw two funeral processions (which looks a whole lot different than what you'd see in the States), did lots of people watching, and took a quick walk through the market as it was the end of the day and most businesses were already closed. We finished at the Cathedral across from the town park and I put aside my fear of heights once again and took them up the several flights of narrow stairs to the bell tower where we enjoyed a beautiful 360° view of the city below us.

On the return to Jicaro, our boat driver took the long way back and gave us a tour through the Isletas. The sun was just beginning to set and the landscape was illuminated in a bright gold hue. Tall palm trees cast their reflections onto the lake's calm water and the artisanal fishermen in their small wooden boats were all returning home for the evening.

***

I had also met a nice young couple from England who were on their honeymoon at breakfast the morning before and talked them into coming with me on the Plantations, Hot Springs and Kayaking tour the following day. On the way to the base of Mombacho volcano, where our tour started, we saw numerous birds and as we approached land, several howler monkeys were hanging out in the trees at the water's edge. Visiting places like Nicaragua and Costa Rica is like going to the zoo, only better, since all the animals are wild and free.

Ask almost anyone who's been to a place with wild animals and they'll all agree, seeing animals in their natural habitats is so very different than going to a zoo where they are encased in a man-made prison.

The first part of the tour was hiking up a hill in the jungle which eventually became flat and cleared to a plantation of plantains (mind you, I still can't tell the difference between plantains and bananas when growing on trees but we were told these were plantains).

From there, we saw a cacao plantation that was being harvested. Several men with machetes were removing the cacao pods from the trees and hacking them open, exposing the beans that would eventually be removed from the pod, sun-dried and turned into chocolate. Once they had enough pods to fill their satchels, they tied them to a donkey and continued to walk up the hill to the next section.

Our next plantation was coffee. I was hoping to see red coffee beans as I knew it was the start of harvest season in Costa Rica but I suppose being further North, Nicaragua's harvest season begins later because the beans were all still green.

We continued to follow the trail to a ranch style home, overlooking the Lake and Islands. Julio set up lunch for us and we sat down at a picnic table to eat our sandwiches and fruit. It was a beautiful setting and in front of us was a large Jicaro tree with gigantic fruits on it.

Heading back down the mountains, the terrain was a little more rough than I anticipated and my cute outdoorsy sandals weren't really holding up well. I hadn't yet replaced my rugged ones yet, since leaving them in the shuttle van in Panama. I'd thought the activities I'd be doing on this trip would all be easy enough without them. I powered through the rest of the tour though, realizing there was nothing I could do at that moment. Taking them off and going barefoot would have been even more painful due to the rough terrain. Plus who knows what type of insect I would have stepped on.

Along the trail, we saw a few large iguanas and howler monkeys as well as more plantations. Arriving at the hot springs, I was happy to take off my shoes and soak them in the warm water. Actually, using warm as a descriptor doesn't really do it justice. This was some of the hottest water I'd ever been in.

Julio told us during the summer months (we were visiting at the tail end of winter), the water's temperature can exceed 70 degrees Celsius. That's about 150 degrees Fahrenheit.

After taking a dip, we walked back to where our boat driver had left the kayaks and lazily made our way down the stream to the mouth of the lake to meet our boat.

The rest of the day was spent chatting with guests, eating and drinking. Mary and Steve invited me to join them for dinner and drinks beforehand and the staff brought us a little tapas while we enjoyed our drinks and watched the sunset from the open-air bar.

Since I was waking up to the sunrise and thoroughly busy during the day, bedtime was always early. I easily fell asleep to the soft sounds of the natural world but awoke to rain, lightning and thunder in the middle of the night. It was a spectacular sight as lightning lit up the night sky surrounding my casita. Since my shutters were open, I watched it for a while but then eventually drifted off again.

***

I wasn't surprised to wake up to the sunrise in the morning. While it often rains at night here, it seems to almost always blow out by morning. That day I was going to Masaya volcano with another couple and was relieved when I saw the sun as it wouldn't have been much fun to peer down into an active volcano if it was raining.

Masaya was about thirty minutes from Granada and getting to the volcano was really easy. You could actually drive right up to the top of the volcano's crater and park there. I guess in Central America, the governments just assume most of the people there will use common sense and not do anything to harm themselves. They're probably less worried about people suing them as well.

Other than Arenal in Costa Rica, (which can only be viewed from the base), I've never been up close to an active volcano so this was very exciting for me. It was probably the one thing I was most looking forward to during my stay at Jicaro. Getting out of the taxi, we could instantly smell the sulfur and see the smoke rising out of the crater. The crater itself was an incredible blend of colors: reds, browns and blacks. Against the blue skies, it was all so vibrant and alive.

There were many birds flying in and out of the crater but I cannot imagine any food sources being able to live down there. Not only was it hot but it smelled really bad. There was however, a quiet stillness to it all and at the same time, an incredible

115

energy, knowing that at any moment this volcano could erupt, shooting ash, lava and rocks out of its massive basin.

We walked to the top of the crater where the Spanish settlers had built a tall cross, hoping to ward off evil spirits as it was thought the volcano was the mouth to hell. They actually named it, "Boca del Infierno". From this vista point, we had a 360° view of the outer lying areas of the volcano and valleys below. It was a beautiful sight to take in. There were very few cars and very few people; this was a sacred space. Perhaps the Spaniard's cross was doing its job and exorcising any evil that tried to enter this natural place.

We could only take the inhalation of the sulfur for a short time and eventually returned down the mountain. Returning to the hotel, I had lunch, hung out in the hammock, did a little work and spent time talking with guests.

I don't know how the Cayuga employees got any work done when they visited the various properties. I spent so much time talking with guests that it was really hard to find time to do any work. I have to admit though, I loved having the opportunity to meet new people and hear about their experiences. One thing that resonated with all of the guests I spoke with was the family vibe you get while staying at Jicaro. The Jicaro Experience was absolutely one of good people, good food, good times, good ambiance. There's nothing better than that when on holiday.

Before returning to my casita that night, I had noticed the blisters on my feet from the day before weren't looking so good. I showed them to Jicaro's assistant manager and a look of concern also came across her face. She told me to wait and returned with an antiseptic gel, Band-Aids and two amoxicillin which were individually sealed.

You know, there were always funny moments on my trips but the amoxicillin had to be one of the more unusual ones. In the States, I would have had to take time off from work, pay $75 to see my doctor, then pay some other ridiculous amount for whatever cream or drug they thought I needed. In Nicaragua, all I had to do was ask the hotel. And really, I didn't even ask for it...it was just provided to me.

Chapter 10
Guiones

"Believe in yourself
Put your troubles on the shelf
Happy to exist
The bad times won't be missed
Don't back down from that wave
You just got to be brave
Everything that you do
Will come back to you
Believe in yourself in every
single way
Have faith in yourself that you
will be OK"
Brian Wilson

Before I left for the airport in the morning to fly to San Jose, I ran into Howard who had stopped by briefly to check in and say goodbye. We enjoyed a quick cup of coffee together and I let him know I fully embraced the Jicaro Experience and was looking forward to returning next year. The chefs had prepared me an egg and cheese breakfast sandwich to go and before I knew it, I was departing the boat and getting into a taxi, returning to Managua airport.

I wasn't quite awake and the coffee hadn't yet kicked in but my taxi driver was extremely talkative and it took all of my energy to try to talk with him in Spanish. All I really wanted to do was look out the window at the pretty countryside scenery we were passing but he wanted to chat and hear about my experiences in his country.

Not wanting to be rude, I did my best to converse with him but also realized I still had a long way to go before I was fully bilingual. The Spanish classes were helping but I really needed the chance to fully immerse myself in the language.

I was flying on Nature Air and had no problems with getting my luggage checked or with the fact that I actually had two carry-ons: a backpack and a small duffel. I flirted a little with the cute guys at the check-in desk and they let it slide. Now that's when speaking Spanish (and being a girl) is really useful.

It's about a seventy-five minute flight to San Jose and when we landed, I was first in line to get through immigration. I didn't know I had to show proof of when I would be leaving the country and so I held up the line as I fumbled in my backpack, looking for my iPod. I had no idea where in my luggage my return flight paperwork was but I figured if I could use the airport's wi-fi, I would be able to log into the Delta app and show them proof of my flight home. When they realized that was the only option, that seemed to be acceptable to them and I then took a taxi to the San Jose hotel where I'd have a quick overnight stay.

I checked in at the hotel and since my room wasn't ready yet (it was only 11 a.m.), I left my luggage at the front desk and walked down to the Cayuga office as they were having their monthly staff meeting. This time, I knew where I was going.

I poked my head in the door of the office and instantly smiled, seeing everyone's friendly faces and knowing I was once again home. While I didn't want to interrupt their meeting, almost instantly everyone stood up to greet me, giving me a hug and kiss, welcoming me back. It's so nice to be embraced by such beautiful people who are all doing good work in the world.

The meeting didn't last long and I walked back to the hotel; it was pouring down rain at this point but I didn't care, it felt good on my skin and the air was warm. I was only at the hotel for one night so I didn't do much in the way of unpacking. I took a quick shower and checked emails before venturing out to meet friends and Cayuga coworkers for dinner.

Michelle had recommended I dress warmly as it would only be about 17 degrees Celsius but I just laughed. First, 17° Celsius is warm for this Northern

California girl and second, I never packed jeans or other warm clothes on these trips – sundresses and sandals only.

In the taxi driving through the streets of San Jose, it was really a wonder that anyone chose to drive there. It was the end of the month and my taxi driver informed me that everyone had gotten paid and was going out for the evening. The traffic was ridiculous.

My driver wasn't sure where he was going and did quite a few maneuvers that had to be illegal, even making his own lane at one point. That was something Troy used to do as well and I'm beginning to understand that maybe that's just the way you drive when you're in the city - on the defensive and making up your own rules as you go.

As a girl who'd lived in the suburbs all her life, this was not something I'd ever had to learn though I doubt similar techniques would be accepted in the States. On the way, we passed by several fast food and chain restaurants. I was surprised and a little sad that the US had so fully infiltrated the city with what I consider to be some of the worst my country has to offer.

After several close calls, we finally found the restaurant. When I saw Michelle, I started laughing because she was in a full Halloween costume. Maria Jose was also dressed up and Michelle had brought costumes for Jennifer and I as well. It was no wonder the owner of the restaurant had seated us upstairs, away from the rest of his patrons that evening.

Dinner was lovely and it was fun to catch up with everyone. Maria Jose was leaving for Marrakech the next day so I was happy to be able to spend a few hours with her before she left. We did a blend of speaking in English and Spanish throughout the evening. While it's good for me to fully immerse into the culture and only be around Spanish speakers, it also takes an enormous amount of energy to try to keep up with them.

***

I knew that I was a very lucky girl to be visiting the Harmony Hotel for the second time in less than 6 months.

The hotel shuttle dropped me off at Pavas Airport but unlike the day before in Nicaragua, I was not so fortunate during the check-in process.

A young woman checked me in and she took her job quite seriously. If only I had waited a few more minutes, I would have been able to check-in with a man and probably flirted my way out of the $40 extra baggage fee. She, however, wasn't going to allow me on the plane with my two small carry-ons (even though the plane was less than half full) and she was definitely going to charge me for the extra piece to be checked. I was bummed but still, I didn't attempt to argue with her. She didn't look as though she'd had any coffee yet and I didn't want to make a scene.

I made my way through the check-in process where they inspected my bags by hand. As I waited to board, I could see the plane through the glass doors and decided to take a photo. I'd had some challenges with my right hand in the past few years, having lost many of the nerve connections.

As I reached for my camera, I lost the grip on it and it fell onto the hard tile floor. You could hear other passengers gasp as I knelt down to pick it up. All was okay though, thank god, as this was a brand new camera and I didn't want to have another loss of a camera this year after losing the new waterproof Sony in June. Thankfully, there wasn't even a scratch on the camera body and the lens was intact.

We had one stop before Nosara in Tambor and I took video of the flight's landings and takeoffs since the original videos were on the camera that was lost in the river. It's a beautiful scene to video, landing and taking off in Tambor, as you're flying right over the water, practically landing on the beach.

Arriving in Nosara, I was greeted by a shuttle driver and we headed out towards Harmony. Just a few weeks before, many of the roads in Nosara had become rivers, having been flooded with the heavy rains they'd been experiencing. I mentally thanked Maria Jose for managing to control the weather and keep the rain at bay for me during this visit.

It turned out that my thanks were just a little premature. The rain did come, shortly after I arrived at the hotel and continued, on and off, for the next two days. It was still warm though and a little bit of rain wasn't going to stop me from enjoying my time at Harmony.

This time when checking in, there was no celebrity to admire but I noticed the nametag of the woman helping me read Irene, who was Harmony's general manager. I was so happy to finally meet her in person. When I was there in June she had been on maternity leave.

The next day I met her husband, Felipe, who worked with Spencer at Experience Nosara. He was taking me and another guest on the Waterfall Hike. While it was an easy hike, it was still a lot of fun and we were able to cross a few small streams, walk through tall grasses, and be amongst the tall trees in the jungle. Fortunately the weather held out for us and the sun was shining the entire time.

On the hike, we were able to experience the different landscapes of the region, seeing several birds and monkeys along the way as well. The two waterfalls were beautiful and the water was refreshing. Felipe was experienced and knowledgeable about the natural world and had brought along a telescopic lens so we could more easily see the wildlife in the canopy of the trees.

Normally, the tour ended with lunch at a local woman's home but she was out that day. Instead we went to a "soda" in the town of Nosara, which was a great cultural experience, one which I highly recommend. I was pleasantly surprised to learn Felipe is also a vegetarian and he was able to confirm the beans at the soda were not made in lard as is often the case at local establishments.

Due to the partially inclement weather the first two days, I did have a little time to work and begin to sort through the thousands of photos I had taken. I was still dealing with my writers block so I didn't get much done in the way of writing other than jotting down notes in my iPod... but I did make every attempt to be clear about what my shorthand meant so I wasn't guessing later on.

In the afternoon, I laid out on my patio's hammock to sort through photos and do a little work. As I was lying there, a large coati walked right up to me. I was so surprised I nearly fell out of the hammock, trying to grab my regular camera for a photo. I don't think the coati realized I was there when he originally decided to walk through my patio because as soon as our eyes met, he became anxious and turned around to walk back in the direction of where he had come from.

I ended up following him to a tree that he climbed but then came down and stood on the sidewalk, staring at me for a moment. I always keep my distance from wildlife, as I didn't want to scare them but I wasn't really sure what this coati was doing or where he wanted to go. He eventually went around another building and disappeared.

Walking back to my bungalow, I heard breaking branches and looked up to see a troop of howler monkeys moving from tree to tree, eventually settling on the trees near the pool. This was a big troop of all ages, including several babies who were clinging to their mom's backs.

There are days when I'm photographing and feel like Alice in Wonderland, going down paths, not knowing where they may lead. I have gotten myself into some precarious situations over the last few years, trying to "get the shot", but I wouldn't change anything. Every scrape, scar and bruise has been worth it.

Having the opportunity to photograph these beautiful animals and share their stories with others makes my life meaningful. And isn't that what life is supposed to be all about it?

***

Since early summer, I'd been talking about surfing in the warm, tropical water of Playa Guiones and the day had finally arrived... one day before my 37th birthday.

Over the past few months, I'd discovered a lot more about training my body/mind, the art of surfing and life in general. Angie had been sending me tips on how to prepare and telling me that I would do great, reminding me to just get out there and have fun.

Chas had me balancing on Bosu balls and Balance Balls, swimming laps in the pool and generally did everything he could to help me stay motivated.

I felt as ready as I could be when Oscar, our surf instructor, met me and another guest, Jordan, at the Harmony lobby. We walked down to the beach and stopped on dry sand for the first part of the lesson. After explaining how to be safe in the water and the correct way to fall off the board (probably the most important thing to know), Oscar drew imaginary surfboards in the sand and showed us how to pop up. Then it was our turn.

It seemed easy enough...on sand. On a board in the rolling waves, I wasn't so sure. Thanks to Chas, I had been doing what he called "burpees with a push up" in the weeks leading up to my trip and if I could do a few sets of those, I knew I could get up to a stand on the board. Staying on it once I was up was a completely different matter.

As we carried our boards out to the water, hesitation came over me as I saw the size of the waves. Oscar must have seen it in my face because he smiled, telling me all would be okay and reminding me that we'd be staying near the white water, where the smaller waves were breaking.

Here's the thing about Mother Nature...you cannot control what she does. I laugh as I write that because giving up control is not easy for me. However, I had no choice when faced with waves that just kept rolling in. Letting go of control was one of the lessons I learned that morning as I got on a surfboard for the first time in my life.

The waves didn't stop; just like life didn't stop. Sure, I could try to put life on pause or shift into neutral but really...it never stops. The world keeps spinning, the tides roll in and out, seasons change, the sun sets and the moon rises. The choice is mine... I could choose to dig my heels in the sand

and get pummeled by the waves (or stung by a stingray on the ocean floor) or I could get out there and do something.

I stood up on the board a few times; I fell down a whole lot more. Really, standing up on it wasn't the problem... riding the wave was the difficult part. Not only did I have to let go of control, I also had to admit I was pretty bad at something.

It was a good reminder that, in life, I had to keep picking myself up, brushing off and taking another step forward to reach my goals. I was winning all over the place; learning to surf but most importantly stepping out of my comfort zone and trying something new.

Oscar was a great source of encouragement; telling me to grab the board (and always be on the right side of it), turn around and get back in. When he could tell I was getting tired of paddling, he'd give me a little extra push to head me in the right direction and then let me know when it was the right moment for me to pop up.

My surfing lesson reminded me that if I truly want to succeed and accomplish my goals, I couldn't ever give up. With effort, courage and support from others, anything is possible.

Only one injury occurred while I was out there, which of course was impressive for me. The scab on my knee from the Balance Ball incident had fallen off the day before and unfortunately, one of the times I popped up, I lost my footing, landing on my knee. The tender skin was just too raw and it started to bleed again, causing both Oscar and Chas to take credit for the resulting scar.

While Angie had originally arranged a private lesson for me, I was actually relieved Jordan was also there and the feeling was reciprocated. It would have been exhausting if he hadn't been. While Oscar was working with Jordan, I had a moment to rest and vice versa. I was also thankful to have Kim there, Jordan's wife, as she took a few photos of us. It was my only physical proof that I actually succeeded in reaching my goal.

Tammy, the director of the Harmony Healing Centre, had arranged for me to have a massage following surfing. What I didn't know was that it would be a couple's massage with Kuki, Harmony's juice bar manager, who I had just met. We found it pretty amusing but the massage was heavenly.

As we finished, we were told to use the showers to rinse off the oil and banana paste, but not to use soap in order to keep the healing properties on the skin and maintain the softness. Both of us commented that post massage we were in a state of bliss and it was only after the shower that we learned the name of the treatment was aptly named, "Banana Bliss". For the rest of the day, our skin was glowing and had a yummy, tropical scent to it.

Tammy had also been so sweet as to arrange a birthday celebration for me that evening. While it was a day before my actual birthday, I normally celebrated my birthday all month so it was the perfect way to begin the festivities.

We decided to meet at Harmony for dinner; after all, they had the best food in town. There were seven of us, including Tammy, Irene, Felipe, Sofia, Kuki, Jorge and me. It was a fun evening with my new friends and a great way to start my 37th year. A year that would bring many new opportunities as well as challenges.

***

The next morning, I woke up to blue skies and sunshine. After all, it was my birthday and the sun always shone on my birthday. I took a walk on the beach, enjoying the solitude and peacefulness, then met Jorge for breakfast. I was pleasantly surprised when the French toast arrived and "Feliz Cumpleaños" was written on the plate. I didn't have any tours planned for the rest of the week so I decided to spend the day doing what I love: photographing our beautiful environment.

As it was nearing low tide, I walked down to the tidepools and found myself enchanted by the loveliness surrounding me.

Waves were crashing against the rocks, pelicans were flying overhead, little fish were swimming in the pools and crabs were quietly trying to blend into the background.

Being enchanted though can lead to unexpected problems... like slipping on the rocks and landing on my tailbone... again. As if it wasn't bad enough that I reopened the wound on my knee the day before while surfing! But, the camera was safe and that was really all that mattered. Of course, after dropping it on the tile floor, I would almost go so far as to say this camera was indestructible (do not try that at home).

When I returned to the hotel, I saw Tammy had sent me an email asking if I'd like to meet in the restaurant for an afternoon snack of fresh watermelon juice and pie. While I normally always go for chocolate, I had actually fallen in love with their banana caramel pie that week.

During our conversation, Tammy and I talked about what brought her to Nosara and Harmony and how her life had been living in Costa Rica the last few years. It was interesting to hear her story, particularly as she sounded a lot like me. What really resonated with me was when she told me that in the past, before having her son, she still always felt like she was so much younger than her actual age.

I often said I still felt like I was twenty-two. While I had a lot of responsibilities, I also maintained quite a bit of freedom. My free spirit persona is one I doubted I'd ever be willing to let go.

When I was with Ethan, I was open to the idea of settling down and becoming more serious about life. Back on my own though, I knew that I enjoyed life on my own terms, with all of its adventures, the ups and downs and everything in between. Of course, I'd prefer if there were more ups, than downs, but you have to take the good with the bad. There's no getting around it.

Jorge and Sophie joined me for dinner later that night and it was the perfect end to a great birthday. I was so happy to be celebrating the day at Harmony. While the Osa Peninsula is one of my favorite places on Earth, Harmony offered a certain sweetness that couldn't really be put into words.

The dessert came with another handwritten note on the plate: Happy Birthday Chrissy.

***

Being in the delightful "land of Harmony", I had completely lost track of not only time but also the date. I realized on my last full day there that I hadn't ventured into town at all. Where had the time gone?

I also realized I had not seen any baby turtle hatchings yet. In speaking with one of the beach security guards, he told me a story about how he was sitting at the beach while working and all of a sudden, the sand below him began to move and out crawled baby turtles.

It is said good things come to those who wait and perhaps it was not yet my time to see the turtles hatch. I reminded myself to be patient. The funny thing about that was that according to earth based religions, the turtle is a totem, symbolizing patient energy.

I knew once I lived there permanently, I wouldn't have such short windows of time to experience everything and perhaps the turtles wouldn't feel so much pressure to hatch.

Turtles are a beautiful reminder to slow down - after all, the turtle is the one who eventually won the race.

There were no more falls or injuries for the remainder of my stay at Harmony, thank goodness. I spent the last few hours of my time there wandering around the property, taking photographs of anything and everything.

In the last week, I had literally spent hours upon hours just being outside and photographing the beautiful environment. Feeling so healthy and free. Time flew by, but Irene caught up with me and insisted I sit down on a lounge chair at the pool, telling me I needed to relax and enjoy my vacation. I still didn't know how to take a vacation. With camera in hand, I was always bopping about, though it was a definite labor of love.

I did oblige her and grabbed a tamarind, lime and ginger drink from the bar before going to the pool. Tamarind is one of my favorite fruit juices; it's slightly sweet and sour at the same time. As instructed, I laid down on a lounge chair but within five minutes, a light rain started. I laughed and cited it as proof that I was not supposed to relax and enjoy my vacation as everyone kept insisting I should.

It only lasted a short time and the sun returned but I had already gotten up and strolled down the path towards the beach, avoiding the main office area so Irene wouldn't catch me.

As I was walking on the path near my bungalow, I heard a strange sawing sound. The hotel was doing construction upgrades in many of the rooms but this sound was coming from high above in the trees.

I looked up to see a squirrel, gnawing his way through a coconut in a palm tree. The coconut was way bigger than the squirrel but he was fixated on getting it open as I'm sure he knew the goodness that awaited him when he finally succeeded. I stood there, totally mesmerized by the squirrel's determination to break open the coconut with its teeth.

After much time, he did end up succeeding and coconut water began to drip out of the fruit onto the ground below. Just like the turtles which didn't make an appearance for me, it was another reminder that good things come to those who not only wait patiently but also work hard to get there. The squirrel epitomized that life lesson for me.

I eventually made it down to the beach and decided to do a little cleanup. It was disheartening to see the trash I found on the beach, either that had been swept onto shore from the ocean or had been left there by someone who didn't care. I did my part to leave that beautiful paradise a little cleaner and prettier. Once I had picked up the trash, I was able to admire the pretty shells, which covered much of the sandy beach.

***

After two weeks of traveling, my suitcase was a bit of a mess and packing had never been one of my strengths. I threw everything in the bag and sat on it as I tried to zip it up.

I was returning to San Jose that morning and had a busy day ahead of me. Irene joined me for my final breakfast at Harmony and she shared stories of her and Felipe's travels in the States. I was grateful to have spent almost a week there and really have the time to get to experience the area.

Just before I left my room to check out, I heard that same sawing sound coming from the tree outside my bungalow. I went out to see if it was the squirrel again but instead, this time, it was a coati.

The squirrel had done most of the work in making a sizeable hole in the coconut and the coati was just finishing it off, now being able to reach inside and take out the "meat". The coati's efforts reminded me of teamwork: that without support from one another, life is so much harder.

While the squirrel had done a lot of the dirty work and the coati benefited from that, relationships and the ability to exist in this world required a certain degree of give and take. I'm sure the coati, in one way or another, would return the favor to the squirrel someday.

The plane ride to San Jose was short, following a different path than the one taken in June. Angie happened to be in San Jose for the week and so I confirmed lunch with her and had the hotel call a taxi for me so I could meet her at the Multiplaza, a gigantic mall in Escazu, with over three hundred stores.

While I had previously said I'd never go to another mall in Costa Rica, it was an easy place for the two of us to meet. We met at the food court, which again was disappointing to see. It was the same as food courts in the States with hundreds of people ordering poor food choices at fast food restaurants like McDonalds, Papa John's and Taco Bell. Angie and I decided to check out a Japanese restaurant at the other end of the mall.

I was grateful for the opportunity to get to know Angie in person as our communications over the last few months had been through email. She was also a vegetarian, which was another pleasant surprise for me as I don't often get to meet too many vegetarians in my travels and this was the second person in just a week.

She had ordered for both of us, however when the bento boxes came, they had chicken in them. Angie had explained to the server that we were vegetarian before ordering and let him know again, when the meals arrived, that we did not want chicken. The server took the boxes away and returned with new ones, without chicken.

I was relieved to learn that it wasn't just me who tried to order vegetarian meals in Costa Rica only to have many of my meals arrive with meat on the plate. Angie said they just didn't understand the concept; thinking it was okay to still put it on the plate and we would just work around it.

As we ate, she shared with me some funny stories about living in Nosara and working at both Harmony and Del Mar Surf Camp. We figured out she was the manager of Harmony when Troy was working there but she had just started and didn't remember him.

Later, I met with some new potential clients and with contracts signed, my portfolio was growing and things were really starting to look up. Maybe, just maybe, I'd be able to move to Costa Rica the next year.

***

In the morning, my breakfast server recommended a local restaurant that I try for lunch and said he could drop me off there once his work day was done.

As we drove through the streets of downtown San Jose, I began to fully understand how easy it would be to hit someone here. There were no painted lines on the roads for lanes much less crosswalks. People just crossed wherever they wanted and it was Jorge's job, as the driver, to maneuver around them.

I always knew the streets in San Jose were a little chaotic but I had never fully experienced them in daylight, especially on a Saturday when most people were off, meeting with friends and shopping.

Jorge dropped me off at the restaurant and introduced me to one of his friends who he said would take care of me. They didn't really have a vegetarian selection but the chefs made do and created a lunch serving of typical gallo pinto. While I waited, I enjoyed a cold beer and did a little people watching. There were both locals and tourists in this establishment and it was decorated with all different types of somewhat strange knickknacks. There were flags hanging from the ceiling, old metal Pepsi-Cola signs, animal heads on wall posts, photos, art and other memorabilia.

I was planning on walking back to the hotel after lunch but decided to take a taxi instead. Not only did the drive there scare me somewhat to consider walking but it also looked like it might start to rain.

In the short ten minute drive back to the hotel, the taxi driver, an extremely religious man, talked to me to about how there was only one God to honor and worship. Not wanting to get into a religious discussion with him, I just nodded my head and tried to figure out how much longer it would be before we arrived back at the hotel.

That night, I reorganized my suitcase to make it more suitable for travel. I had only purchased a few bags of coffee as gifts for people back home but I was unable to get my suitcase to close. After rearranging the pieces many times, I eventually got it zipped up and set my alarm for 5:00 a.m. My flight out of San Jose was at 8:00 and I was told we had to leave for the airport by 5:30.

Other than my lip gloss and Burt's Bees antibacterial spray being confiscated at the gate (not at security, mind you), the flight home was insignificant. I did however complain to Delta Airlines about the confiscated items a few weeks later and they gave me 10,000 miles for my Skymiles account. Of course, if I had just stuck them in my jacket pocket, they never would have known. Security is somewhat hit or miss there. They're

super strict about some things, like lip gloss in
backpacks, but not other things, like checking
jacket pockets.

Chapter 11

Harmony

"Time spent with cats is never wasted."

Sigmund Freud

Returning home, I was, once again, immediately ill. As soon as I stepped out of SFO, my nose started to run and my eyes were watering. It was also unbearably cold compared to the last two weeks of tropical travels.

It would suck for the next forty-seven days until I left for Cuba. It seemed like my health condition worsens in cold weather and it was definitely winter, at this point, in Northern California.

Just like before, I had to regroup and refocus, remembering what was important. Especially since my goal of moving to Costa Rica was so much closer. With Thanksgiving just around the corner, I wrote down some of the things I was grateful for, hoping to remind myself of all that I already had and what I was looking forward to...

I am grateful for those people who believed in me, supported me and helped me reach my goals this year. I would not be where I am today if it were not for the help of others who stood by me and saw the potential in me to succeed.

I am grateful for the experiences I have when I travel and get to meet new people from different parts of the world. Meeting them has opened my eyes to new ways of thinking and living and gives me the chance to share their stories with others, making our big world a little smaller.

I am grateful that today I caused no physical suffering to any other living being, direct or indirect by choosing to only eat foods that come from our Earth.

141

I am grateful for the many opportunities that have presented themselves to me this year.

I am grateful for good food, beautiful surroundings and the kindness of strangers.

***

Shortly after this day of thanks, my sweet little cat Harmony, who was 16 at the time, became ill. Just after falling asleep, I woke up to find him sitting next to me, trying to purr but unable to. It was a horrible scene to watch. Every time he purred, he'd have a violent gagging attack. Harmony had always been known for his purr.

At midnight, realizing it wasn't a one-time incident, I called the emergency animal hospital and they said since he was continuing to eat and act normally, other than the purring, that I could probably wait until morning.

I couldn't sleep that night and I dragged through my workout with Chas but like the nurse said, there was probably nothing that could be done until the vet's office opened at 7:30.

At least working out with Chas gave me a break from the overwhelming sadness I was feeling while I tried to comfort Harmony. Especially since my comforting him only seemed to make things worse as he would then try to purr. It was a vicious cycle. The vet's initial reaction was that he just had a sore throat but a week later, with the problem continuing, I was advised to take him to a specialist for an endoscopy.

It turned out that Harmony had a rare condition called laryngeal paralysis. It's more common in dogs which explains why his regular vet didn't know about it. She admitted that in her twenty-four years of being a vet, she had never treated a cat with it before. Why these bizarre occurrences happen to me is still an unknown.

He was only paralyzed on the left side of his larynx so they couldn't do a surgery, which may have helped in the long run. I didn't know what to do.

The specialist told me that when he tried to purr and couldn't, while he would get frustrated, it probably wasn't a source of pain or suffering for him.

While I'm sure she is good at what she does, she wasn't exactly the most compassionate vet I had met. This was confirmed when she told me bluntly he'd never be the same cat again and I should give my petsitter a written directive in case he became more sick while I was in Cuba. The tears turned into uncontrollable sobbing at that point.

He had been healthy for so many years leading up to this point and this news broke my heart. Until now, there had never been any doubt he'd come along with me on the journey of moving to Costa Rica.

I had done all the research: finding out what size carrier I needed, how much it would cost to fly with him, whether or not the Admiral's Club would allow him in the club on the layover, what Costa Rica's requirements for pet entry were and that the apartments I was looking at allowed pets. I had also figured out everything I needed to bring for him on this move: his litter box, litter, food, bed, toys and of course kitty treats.

Such horrible sadness embodied me during this time. While the vets said he probably wasn't suffering, I knew Harmony and I knew that his quality of life had changed. Purring was one of the main things he did all day. Eat, sleep, purr.

Worse, every night, he'd try to curl up next to me but couldn't. He'd become frustrated and physically upset as he walked to the other side of the bed. This would happen throughout the night so neither of us was getting much sleep. I knew I couldn't make a major, life-changing decision on no sleep so I decided not to do anything until after I returned from Cuba. I just prayed he was okay while I was gone.

Chapter 12
¡Cuba!

"When you think things are bad,
when you feel sour and blue,
when you start to get mad...
you should do what I do!
Just tell yourself, Duckie,
you're really quite lucky!
Some people are much more...
oh, ever so much more...
oh, muchly much-much more
unlucky than you!"
Dr. Seuss

Despite the more recent hints the Universe had given me about visiting Cuba, I'd had a keen interest in traveling there for several years now. It really began once I started doing photography work and learning more about interesting places to shoot. And from what I imagined, Cuba would be one very interesting place to shoot.

About half the people I knew were horrified that I was going (mostly those in the US) and the other half were excited (mostly those in Costa Rica and Canada). I told the horrified ones to just wait until I returned. I'm sure there were still whispers of "Chrissy's gone loca".

The most commonly asked questions leading up to the trip were "Are you traveling through Cancun or the Caymans?" and "Why would you want to visit a communist country?"

I went there legally...I had an approved US State Department issued Visa. I traveled on a charter flight out of Miami Airport on Delta Airlines to Havana and returned the same way. The restrictions have been lifted (to a certain degree) for travel to Cuba. The caveat is you must travel with an approved tour company on a "people to people" tour. What that means is I wasn't going to be wandering off on my own to explore or go snorkeling in the Caribbean Sea (as it was not a "people to fish" tour), though we were fortunate to visit the beach one afternoon as a group.

As for visiting a communist country, I'd read The Communist Manifesto by Karl Marx and Frederick Engels in Graduate school and I actually liked a lot of what Marx and Engels had to say. I knew there were definite downsides to communism in practice, however the underlying aspect of socialism intrigued me and I wanted to learn more. And really, I wanted to see and experience it firsthand.

From a photojournalist's standpoint, it was like stepping back in time. For the first part of the trip, we stayed at the 5-star Hotel Nacional de Cuba (note: 5-stars for Cuban standards, not US) which was built in 1930 and is where Sinatra and Gardner, Nat King Cole, the mafia and many others all stayed during the "heyday" years, prior to the Revolution and the Missile Crisis.

I learned that it was the location of where the missiles were to be launched in 1961 (which was not so cool but still a piece of history to learn about). I also wanted to see our old 1950's cars cruising down the Malecón, listen to jazz, explore Habana Viejo and so much more...

I had created a "Cuba Bucket List" before arriving:

Drink a mojito where Hemingway hung out
Go to the beach
Attend a baseball game
Smoke a cigar (which I don't condone doing normally but hey, it was Cuba.)
Visit the John Lennon statue
Meet artists and buy their art and music
Make new connections, both within the group and with the Cuban people
Eat at the Las Terrazas vegetarian restaurant

Learn more about socialism and Cuba's history
Visit their natural environment
Watch people playing chess in the park
Stay at the Hotel Nacional
Watch street performers
Visit a Cuban market
Spend the night with a cute Cuban man, preferably a
baseball player

I know, that last item would be challenging considering I was on a tour where there was very little free time but this was a "people to people" tour after all and that might give me the opportunity to meet a man, or at least, I hoped it would.

***

As the airport shuttle was entering the freeway near my house, I could see a sign on the front of a building which said, "Escape". That was what I was doing, albeit only for a week. I was finally getting away from reality and the constant work on my plate.

With very little access to the internet in Cuba, I was ready to fully embrace being technology free for a week. I was sure if there was an internet café available, I'd probably take the opportunity to post something on Facebook and make my friends envious of my adventures but other than a few minutes here and there, I was pleased to be leaving technology in my rearview.

I was also escaping from my sadness and frustration with my ongoing relationship issues in the States. I tried to explain to work, family, etc that it was only a matter of time before my health issues overtook my mental state as I was already feeling unstable but they just didn't get it.

I was certain that for the next eight days, I'd be able to breathe again, being in a warmer, more humid environment, which would be a welcome, though short, reprieve from the misery I experienced every day at home. It was the recharge I needed since I had been miserably sick since returning from the last trip to Central America.

***

When I arrived in Miami, I was in a bit of a daze. With my tailbone still severely injured from my falls in October and November, I slept very little on the plane and had to get from the American terminal to the Delta one.

A nice man took pity on me and offered to give me a ride on his cart to the main entrance of the AA terminal. I'm guessing that I must have looked really tired. I still had to walk the rest of the way to the Delta terminal but at least I was saved walking what seemed like 60 gates worth of space.

Finding the Delta terminal, I still wasn't sure where I was supposed to be. I had been told by the tour company there would be multiple lines of people checking in and to ask someone which line I should be in. I asked the woman at security, showing her my flight information and she told me to go downstairs. That advice seemed odd since I was standing in front of the ticket counters but I did as I was told.

However, getting downstairs, the only thing I could see was baggage claim carousels. No one was around, as no flights were coming in at that moment. I finally found someone who looked like she worked for the airline and again showed her my ticket. Of course, she told me to go upstairs. I explained that I was sent downstairs and then it came to her. She explained that I needed to go to the end of the terminal on the first floor. There, she told me, I would find the check in counters for the charter flights.

That was what was missing from the woman's instructions upstairs: go to the end of the terminal which was such a far walk from where I was that I couldn't even see the signs in the distance.

There appeared to be only one line so I assumed that was the one I needed. I was surrounded by Cubans with multiple pieces of luggage, most of which were wrapped in neon green plastic wrap to prevent theft but I could still make out what they were bringing in: Christmas gifts. It was, after all, Christmas Eve. Some people had big screen TV's, others had furniture and game systems. I saw some people with toilet paper and realized then I had forgotten the roll I had wanted to bring, just in case the public restrooms didn't have any.

After about thirty minutes, I finally realized I wasn't in the right line and had to check in first at a desk on the far side of the room to pick up customs paperwork for when I arrived in Cuba. The terminal was really poorly laid out, as this desk should have been at entrance so everyone could see it but instead was on the opposite side, hidden by all the people in line. The instructions they had provided to me also failed to mention a desk that had customs paperwork on it that needed to be filled out. My inner control freak was resisting the urge to let someone have a piece of my mind.

There had been so much paperwork that was originally mailed to us. I'd had to read and sign pages upon pages of documents. I just don't understand why the charter company, who was responsible for handing out this additional paperwork, just couldn't have included it in the original mailing. Or, at the very least, mentioned we needed to pick up the paperwork and fill it out before getting in the line to check-in.

There was a woman who had been walking around making announcements and possibly she had said something about the paperwork but she only spoke in Spanish and talked much too fast for me to catch any of what she said.

Since I had been standing in line for such a long time, I made new friends who offered to watch my bag for me and save my place. This was fortunate since I had to get back in the same line after getting the forms and the line had now doubled in size behind us. The line was moving slowly because people were checking so much luggage and it all had to be weighed and paid for.

The luggage fees were different for charters for Cuba. You were allowed one piece of luggage up to forty-two pounds and it cost $1 for every pound over. I finally made it up to the front of the line and the agent asked if I was able to sit in the emergency row. I was happy to oblige her. Emergency rows are the best in coach as they offer so much more leg room and after a cramped red eye, I was relieved to get a little extra room, even if it was only an hour long flight. I asked her for a window seat and was relieved to learn one was available.

Meanwhile, her colleagues were trying to take my carry-on and put it on the scale but I kept insisting I was taking it on the plane with me and not checking any luggage. I wasn't so worried about theft; I was more worried about what baggage claim would be like in Cuba. The airline employees kept staring and pointing at my bag, which I will admit was a little large but it would fit. Or, I would make it fit.

After all, it had just traveled across country with me in the overhead bin so I didn't foresee any problems with taking it on the next leg of my flight. They were whispering to each other in Spanish but I didn't care. I wasn't going to check my bag.

Even though I wasn't checking any luggage, I still had to pay some sort of tax at yet another ticket counter. I don't know what it was for and since it was only a few dollars I decided not to question it. I really just wanted my ticket and to get back upstairs, through security and find a place that served breakfast. I desperately needed a cup of coffee.

Security, surprisingly, was a breeze to get through. There were only two other people in front of me in line and it was Christmas Eve morning, one of the busiest days of the year for travel.

My only options for breakfast near the gate were Starbucks and Cinnabon. I wasn't about to break my ban on Starbucks and Cinnabon did not sound good to me. So I wandered around, dragging my luggage with me, hoping to find someplace with just a cup of coffee and bagel. I eventually did find a little deli but really wasn't satisfied, knowing this would be my last real meal for an entire week.

The plane we were on was a large 737 with forty-eight rows, six across. I suppose it had to be big given the amount of cargo being brought in by the travelers. Yet another reason I was happy to have my luggage in the overhead. I could easily exit the plane, get through immigration and customs and not have to wait and sort through everyone's luggage and Christmas gifts to find my one small bag.

The flight time was forty-six minutes and had I paid for it, it probably would have been the most expensive flight I'd ever taken, considering the short distance. I didn't do the dollar per mile calculation exactly but it sure seemed astronomical to me. Charter flights to Cuba are approximately $550 and the distance is about 200 miles. Fortunately, I didn't have to pay for the flight outright, as the tour company was offering a special when I signed up with flight included.

***

Walking down the steps of the plane to the tarmac, it reminded me of my travels to Costa Rica and Nicaragua. The warm, tropical air defrosting my body from the cold winter that had just begun in Northern California.

Stepping off the last stair, I was mindful of my feet and where I was. I was now on communist soil in a country in which an embargo had been in effect since 1962...almost fifty years. I knew at some point in the future, the US would lift the embargo and the Cuba that is today would not be the same Cuba people will visit in the future. I wanted to know and see firsthand this piece of history before it changed. Still, getting back to the moment of disembarking, their soil felt pretty much the same as our soil.

As I walked into the terminal, I knew my stubbornness over not checking my bag had been the right call. I quickly made my way through immigration, which was a narrow booth with a locked door on the opposite side which the agent had to buzz me through once the transaction was complete. She also took my photo from a small camera that was hanging from the ceiling of the booth.

I did have to go through another set of security checks before getting to the baggage carousels, putting my luggage on a small conveyor belt and walking through a metal detector. I couldn't really understand why I was then also wanded by a female agent since the metal detector didn't go off but I didn't take it personally. Perhaps the metal detectors didn't actually work and they just want to give the appearance to people that they were functional? Although we were entering the country, not exiting, so I wasn't too sure what security risk we presented.

While I still had to wait for the rest my group to find their bags, I was able to go outside and soak up the warm humid sunshine, taking in my first glimpses of the country.

Immediately, I noticed the old cars from the States. I was blown away as the first ones I saw were in such good condition with impeccable paint jobs and really clean exteriors. I also noticed all of the people waiting outside for their loved ones to get through customs.

I found Margarita, our tour guide for the week, and she explained to me many of these people hadn't seen their relatives in many years, sometimes more than twenty or thirty. There was so much joy and beautiful embraces being exchanged between family members and friends.

Driving on the streets of Havana, I immediately noticed a stark difference from the United States: Cuba's billboards. While our billboards in the States are generally advertising something we should buy (based on our capitalist ideals) like a disgusting $0.99 hamburger at one of the many fast food restaurants people like to frequent, Cuba's billboards were notably political and many of them were reminders of the past; the revolution, their heroes, political signs and mantras like Viva La

Revolucion or my favorite, Socialismo o Muerte. I would learn later that Patria o Muerte (Country or Death) is their national motto and there were signs all around with this slogan: on large billboards, painted on walls and even some just handwritten on pieces of paper and taped to doors, windows and balcony railings.

Sadly, I had no idea what the US's national motto was and had to look it up when I returned home: In God We Trust. That seemed so odd to me. While "Patria o Muerte" is, well, a little revolutionary and aggressive, "In God We Trust" seems to go against the policy of separation of church and state.

Some of the signs I was seeing, I just didn't understand. I was able to translate them but I wasn't able to identify with what they signified.

Such as this one...

"We see you pure as a child, pure as a man, Comandante Che, friend"

I asked Joa, my friend who has traveled to Cuba several times about this and she told me it most likely is a billboard in honor of Che Guevara and his ideas. It didn't hold much meaning for me but it clearly did for the Cuban people. I thought of the various airports, libraries and parks named after political heroes back in the states but found that honor less impactful than the billboards.

Another thing I couldn't help but observe was that the Cuban flag was everywhere: restaurants, hanging off the sides of tall buildings, outside of homes, inside of homes, seriously, everywhere. It was even hanging in the back of our shuttle (which, I'll mention here, was made in China).

Room check-in at Hotel Nacional wasn't until 4 p.m. so we stopped at a local Paladar for lunch. Paladares are privately owned restaurants in Cuba, normally in the owner's home. It was a lovely restaurant, probably their living room at one point, and the food was okay, but really overpriced, especially for their vegetarian fare.

It was a set menu, cost me about $20 and consisted of a mojito (my first ever), spinach soup that was more broth than veggies, cooked cabbage (a food I despise), a few carrots and cucumbers. I don't even spend that much money on soup, salad and a drink here in California and was pretty shocked that I was spending that much in Cuba.

Most of the meals on the tour were included with the price but going to a Paladar was not since it wasn't government run. One reason for the expense might have been the fact that the owners were not entitled to the same discounts that government-owned restaurants were given at the markets.

Of course, it could also have been just a blatant attempt to rip off tourists visiting from the US. In researching this online, it seems there are quite a few shady deals happening to overcharge tourists and make a few extra bucks. It was an interesting experience though and a sign of what was to come.

It was also a good opportunity to meet the other people on the tour. There were two other families traveling with me. One was a mom and son who were celebrating their 90th birthday (a cute way of saying that the mom, Sara, was turning 60 and her son, Daniel, was turning 30). The other group was a family of five. Lindsay and Mike, the parents and their kids: Ben, 21, Nathan, 18 and Natalie, 15. They were all great to travel with and I loved getting to know them.

Not really having a family of my own at the moment and it being the holidays, these seven people would become my surrogate family over the next seven days. I really enjoyed getting to know each of them and we all agreed that at some point, we'd have a reunion in either Nicaragua or Costa Rica. I promised them that the food and hotels would be much better than those in Cuba.

We finally arrived at the hotel and while there was so much interesting history, it was somewhat rundown. It was supposed to be a 5-star hotel but we would quickly learn that 5 stars in Cuba was about 3 stars in the United States. Their check-in procedures were terrible. If I thought "Tico Time" was slow in Costa Rica, Cuban time was ten times slower.

The hotel itself needed major renovations. The carpets were stained, torn and worn down. The showerhead in my room barely put out any water and it sprayed it in every possible direction, except down.

I thought I'd take a quick nap before dinner but when I pulled the sheets down on the first bed, I noticed what looked like a blood stain. I went to the second bed and didn't bother to look. I knew this was just something I was going to have to deal with for the next few days. I did catch a glimpse of the comforter though and quickly closed my eyes, trying to put what I saw out of my head.

This was such a different experience than the ones I've had at the Cayuga hotels these last few years. Over the next week, I became so much more appreciative of the quality lodging and service I had received in other parts of the world.

Dinner that night was interesting. We sat down and the first thing I noticed was the body of a whole pig roasting on a spit a few feet away from us. We then all received a welcome mojito drink and what looked like plantain chips. So, other than the pig, it started off pretty good, but then the meal came.

I first received a small plate with cabbage, tomatoes and cucumbers on one side of it. The rest of the meal was family style and it appeared our options were either chicken or pork. When the beans and rice finally appeared, the beans were in a large bowl that was more liquid than beans.

Over the course of the week, I had to enact a policy of "don't ask, don't tell" when it came to that liquid because I was sure it wasn't vegetarian. I then got my "special vegetarian" meal which was a plate of cabbage, tomatoes and cucumbers; the same as the small plate, only larger.

I really dislike cabbage, but cabbage it was, and it was cabbage all week long. Never again do I want to eat, or even see, cabbage.

Thankfully the people and the connections we were making made up for the bad food. A group of musicians played in the background as we all talked and got to know one another better. Every time Lindsay spoke, she sounded exactly like my Aunt Jacci, even her laugh was the same.

Being three hours behind on California time, I had a difficult time getting to sleep that night. I was definitely tired from traveling and not sleeping on the redeye into Miami but I was also excited and wide awake, thinking about all that was to come in the next seven days. We weren't given an itinerary until we landed so I had been eagerly awaiting the piece of paper to tell me what we'd be doing.

Chapter 13

Havana

"I know, up on top you are seeing great sights, but down here at the bottom we, too, should have rights."

Dr. Seuss

Waking up that first morning in Cuba, I felt like a kid on Christmas morning. Oh wait, it was Christmas morning! I had purposefully planned this trip around the holidays, not wanting to spend them by myself. It was 5 a.m. when I woke up and at about 6:00, I looked outside but it was still totally dark. I kept checking the clock on my iPod thinking maybe the clocks were wrong as there was no sign of daylight from any of the windows.

Shortly after 7:00 though, I started to see the first rays of light and ran outside. As the sun rose, it lit up the back of the hotel and cast a golden hue on all of the buildings facing the Malecón.

The Malecón is a long esplanade in Havana and the sidewalk on the waterfront side is often used as a hangout spot for people of all ages. As I walked around the property, I saw several peacocks and peahens as well as a few strange looking birds. They looked similar to a turkey but had tiny black and white polka dots on them. They were also really feisty, chasing after one another on the grassy lawn. I couldn't tell if they were angry with each other, maybe one was trying to steal the other's mate or if it was some type of weird mating ritual.

In the interest of not being too repetitive, let me just say that for the most part, all of the meals in Cuba were "interesting". Breakfast was a buffet offered at the hotel. I generally don't like buffets as the food isn't freshly prepared and this one was no exception. There was a huge assortment of prepared foods available along with a crepe station, omelet station and other egg preparation stations. There were also fruit and bread stations. Some of the food appeared to be from the previous night's dinner. Not repurposed... just reheated like leftovers.

They had two types of coffee: Cubana coffee in a thermos which I had and then coffee made in a vending machine (like the ones you might see at schools, hospitals and car dealerships). Lindsay tried the coffee made in the machine because the thermos had run out and said it was the worst coffee she had ever tasted. Mine, on the other hand, was delicious, which prompted her to throw out the bad coffee and wait for the good stuff. I was baffled as to why they would even choose to serve such horrible coffee.

While still a little jetlagged, I was jazzed about all that we'd be doing that day. First on the schedule was touring the streets of Habana Viejo. As we drove along the Malecón, heading towards Old Havana, we took in our first real glimpses of this unknown country. While we saw some of Havana yesterday, it was all in a bit of a haze, having no time to settle before beginning the tour.

Driving along the Malecón, it reminded me of an unmaintained 19th Avenue in San Francisco. In Cuba, there were all of these great homes, townhomes and even a few small high-rises throughout the cities but none of them had been maintained for fifty years so they were all deteriorating. It was really quite sad because the architecture and colors could have been so beautiful.

With the embargo from the US (or "blockade" as the Cubans call it), they are unable to get materials, or the funds needed, to make repairs.

While it was Christmas, there were still a lot of people out and about in the town square area setting up a swap meet of books and music. As we walked through the streets and down alleys, the architecture changed from San Francisco's 19th Avenue to that of New Orleans, with pretty colors, storefronts on the first floor with hotels and apartments on the higher levels and balconies overlooking the avenues with laundry hanging off the railings.

We came to one section that had been completely restored with buildings facing a huge open square and a fountain in the middle. Kids and families were hanging out near the fountain, people were walking their dogs, one child was roller skating. From the look on this face, most likely putting his brand new Christmas gift to good use.

We continued walking and passed by a gun museum. Unlike the rights afforded to US citizens by the second amendment, no private citizens in Cuba have guns. Only the military has the legal right to the own them although I'm sure there is still crime and an illegal gun market.

In the Happy Planet Index, Costa Rica is #1 and Cuba ranks at #7 for having the happiest most sustainable people in the world. The US (I'll repeat) ranks at #114. I found it really fascinating that Cuba ranked so highly since they were still going through issues with food rationing and not having enough supplies.

I would much rather live in a society that doesn't allow guns or use my taxes to support wars and train a military to kill people.

I may be naïve when I say that but I really do love John Lennon's idea of "living life in peace". Costa Rica doesn't have a military, Cuban people don't have guns and they both have some of the happiest people in the world, living in some of the most sustainable countries in the world. There has to be a correlation. Especially since both countries put more money towards health and education than they do military expenditures.

Cuba promotes socialism and a lack of competition, which could be why they made the top 10 of the happiness index? While not technically a socialist country, Costa Rica also offers free education and healthcare to its citizens. (And neither country, as of 2011, has a Starbucks. Just saying...)

I wondered what would happen in Cuba if the embargo/blockade was removed and those in the US could travel to Cuba legally and with ease? What if Cuba could receive goods and supplies at cheaper prices and more easily from our manufacturers?

They still wouldn't have access to certain things like satellite TV and cable; the government would still control what activities from the outside world were available to them. They probably still wouldn't have internet in their homes without being monitored and having to pay a heavy expense, beyond the $20 per month that they make on average.

If they had access to more things, would capitalism then begin to slowly infiltrate the country? What would happen to their socialist ideals? Socialism and capitalism are such loaded words for so many people. I found these two quotes, which are at opposite ends of the spectrum:

"Socialism is a philosophy of failure, the creed of ignorance, and the gospel of envy, its inherent virtue is the equal sharing of misery." Winston Churchill

"More socialism means more democracy, openness and collectivism in everyday life." Mikhail Gorbachev

I still felt torn on the choice between the two philosophies. I favored a balance of capitalism and socialism but was unsure how that could possibly be obtained.

We came up to a large Cathedral, again very old and desperately needing repairs and a paint job. It had a large nativity scene outside and inside, Christmas mass was happening. It was all in Spanish so I didn't understand most of it but it seemed like they were reciting the Our Father prayer.

From 1967 – 1997, Fidel Castro had declared Cuba an atheist country and very few religious holidays were celebrated or acknowledged. I was told those measures were taken because religious holidays like Christmas interfered with the sugar cane harvest and also promoted commercialism (a no-no in Cuba).

However, in 1997, the Pope was considering a visit to Cuba and Castro decided the country would no longer be atheist, and instead become Catholic. There was a decorated Christmas tree in the church and one in Hotel Nacional as well. I also saw Christmas trees in several homes as we walked by them.

We then went to Hemingway's hangout, La Bodeguita del Medio and drank mojitos (yes, it was only 10 a.m. but they were handing them out and this was on my bucket list). The bar was packed full of people and a group of musicians were playing in the corner.

I was standing next to a man at the bar who was sitting in front of a typewriter. He asked me for my name and after I told him, he started to type a letter to me. I had to pay him $5 for the letter but he was an older man and while it was a bit of a tourist trap, I obliged him. The piece of paper he typed it on was on the letterhead of La Bodeguita del Medio, with his photo on one side and what looked like a photo of a coin with Hemingway's head on the other side. He signed it with his initials, OL. His name was Orlando Laguardia, "poeta de la Bodeguita del Medio".

Perhaps someday his letter will be famous. It was a sweet poem and a nice gift to remember him by.

As we walked through the streets, I began to notice how everything, even the little things, were really old. The cash register at the gun museum had to be at least fifty years old and the typewriter Orlando had typed my poem on was the same. The general population didn't have access to much of anything new and current.

We were asked by people dressed in bright colors and holding large cigars if we wanted to take our picture with them, or just a picture of them, for cash. I understand that's how they're trying to make money but I imagined how strange it would feel to have tourists wandering through my city and taking photos of me, as if I were on display or in existence purely for their amusement and as such, decided not to take part.

I also never haggled. If I purchased something and the vendor told me it cost $5, I handed over $5. $20, $40, it didn't matter. It was about the principle.

First of all, what they were selling was their art, their creation. They worked hard to create it and I didn't want to discount their talents. Secondly, compared to me and probably you, these people had so very little. Sure, sometimes things were overpriced but if I really wanted it, it was worth the sticker price. I wouldn't walk into Target and negotiate with the cashier, so I didn't feel it was an acceptable practice in other countries either.

Margarita then took us to Callejón de Hamel (Hamel's Alley) which is a community project promoting Cuban art, music and culture. Though it was a very small space and they didn't charge admission, it had thrived for the last twenty years, being a visual manifestation of the founder, Salvador González's goal to highlight the Afro-Caribbean culture and create a place for all to come to appreciate art, music and culture. It was a place for children and adults to be taught the creative arts and be given the opportunity to express themselves creatively.

Besides the art and music, there was a strong emphasis on Santeria, a religion many Cubans followed. The main premise, from what I could understand from the brief introduction I received, was that we had to be one with our spirit; one with our mind and heart. People who followed the Santeria religion dressed in white and wore beaded necklaces, for at least the first year as they were being initiated. The religion originated in West Africa and while its premise shared some themes with yoga, I learned later that animal sacrifice was common in the Santeria religion. That would not be a yoga practice, but the oneness, and the being one with spirit, was comparable.

Lunch was at La Torre Restaurant, on the top floor of an old apartment building. On the 32nd floor, it had an incredible 360° view of Havana and the Caribbean Sea. Going up the elevator though, I was slightly claustrophobic and also anxious about the potential of it breaking down. Even Hotel Nacional's elevator, which only had a few floors, made me nervous. It would make strange sounds as it descended and often, when waiting for it, the numbers would skip.

At La Torre though, I was even more worried as we had thirty-two floors to traverse and no sign posted as to when it was last maintained. I also noticed there was no emergency phone or any way of contacting someone if the elevator were to break.

The elevator doors finally opened, I was able to breathe again and thankfully we were immediately offered a welcome drink. I was surprised when they handed us Cuba Libres.

A Cuba Libre is made with rum, lime juice and cola and translated as "Free Cuba". My assumption had been that the drink had originated in the States as a way of supporting the Cuban people who were under an authoritarian's rule, so being offered one in Cuba was a little bizarre.

My travels taught me that many Cubans do feel like they're free and the actual origin of the drink's name was unknown. There were, of course, many stories and groups who claimed it but in any case, its first known origin dated back to the early 1900's, before Castro was even born.

Sitting down to eat, Margarita still didn't know what to do with me and my strange eating habits so she offered me an omelet. I generally don't eat eggs at home but when traveling, it is often times the only way to get protein so I conceded. I had a cheese omelet with, of course, cooked cabbage on the side. There were also cooked carrots and rice but no beans. I was finding that meals were not only interesting in Cuba, the food combinations were also a little odd.

We then drove to Revolution Square to take photos but what we were all more interested in were the large depictions of Che on the side of one building and a man who looked just like Jesus on another across from the monument. The other man was not Jesus. I'm not sure if any of us ever fully understood who really was depicted there.

As we were standing in the parking lot, I noticed a billboard across the street, which mentioned the 50-some years of struggles and successes for Cuba and there was just too much irony in it not to take a photo of it while an old 1950's car drove past.

It really was like Cuba was suspended in time, living in the 1950's. They were never able to move into the future and were stuck, not knowing any other way to live as they'd been cut off from the world for so many years. It explained why black and white photos of the country today still looked authentic; like they were taken before color photography existed.

Our last activities of the day were to meet a local artist, Ruben Fernandez Leal, who lived across the street from Margarita and visit John Lennon's statue in a nearby park (the latter being a special request I had made earlier in the day).

Ruben invited us into his home and showed us his works of art. He spoke with us about his life, his art and his dreams, one of which was to obtain a Visa to visit Sacramento, California for an exhibit of his art in May 2012. When he learned I lived only a few hours away, he invited me to be his guest. While I was probably going to be living in Costa Rica by that time, it was still a kind gesture.

The art created by Ruben was so dynamic. He would take a piece of canvas, paint on it and then attach thin strips of wood to the canvas, with painted images on both sides of the wood so when you looked at it from either side, it became a three dimensional piece of art. I purchased a small piece that had a moon painted on one side of the wood pieces and the sun painted on the other.

From there, we walked over to the park where I had read there was a statue of John Lennon. The park was located in the Vedado District of Havana and was often called "John Lennon Park".

Unfortunately our guide called it just Lennon Park when she told the rest of the group where we were going and there were a few appalled looks in response. Lennon and Lenin sounded exactly the same and it was almost comical to mix up peace-loving John Lennon for the Russian tyrant, Vladimir Lenin. Thankfully, the sculpture itself sorted us out.

It was life-sized with Lennon sitting on a bench, made of bronze. On the ground at his feet was the inscription: *"Dirás que soy un soñador pero no soy el único"* (You may say I'm a dreamer, but I'm not the only one). While he did not have his signature round glasses on (we were told they had been stolen and vandalized many times), there was a park security guard who came over with a pair so the photo would be complete.

We had a few hours to rest at the hotel before dinner and I took that time to wander around the property, check out the pool (but not actually sit down) and check my emails.

The hotel only offered wifi on its executive floors but did have a business center that other guests could use for a small fee. Its computers and internet service had to be some of the slowest available anywhere. I'm sure if there were speakers hooked up to the computer, I would have heard that old familiar tune from when I was first on dialup in the mid-90's.

Margarita told us that while the "internet cable" was only twelve miles from the shores of Cuba, it belonged to the United States and therefore, Cuba was not allowed access to it. Instead, they somehow received internet service from Venezuela and that cable was only installed within the last year or so. I had always thought we got internet through surface cables or satellites so these underwater cables were really beyond my understanding.

Dinner was at La Divina Pastora, near Parque Morro Cabana. We were given another welcome drink that was a bright blue color and served in a martini glass. There was some debate over whether or not it contained any alcohol and if there was, it had to be such a very small amount because I didn't feel a buzz. Since I didn't normally drink hard alcohol, I figured it was safe to assume that I would be the first to feel the effects of the drink.

Margarita and I had more problems as I attempted to order what I thought would be a simple meal. All I was asking for was a plate of rice and beans, but for some strange reason, the restaurant had no beans. I just could not understand that. Beans were one of the most common staples, if not the most common staple, in all of Cuba.

Then, since fish is often confused as "not meat", they brought me a plate with two shrimp on it as an appetizer. I returned that and the server then brought me a small plate of cucumbers, beets, carrots and green beans and an entrée consisting of a cheese omelet, cauliflower and rice.

They also didn't have Cristal's, which I thought was odd since it was a national beer. It took me a few more days, but I'd eventually figure out that with Cuba's rationing system and limited access to food and beverages, they just didn't have the ability to properly provide for its citizens, much less its tourists.

After dinner, we drove to the nearby fort to watch the Cannon Blast Ceremony. It was interesting to take part in but not something I'd do again if I were to return to Cuba. The ceremony took place every night at exactly 9 p.m. All of the lights were turned off at the fortress and men, dressed up in historical costumes kind of like those you'd see at Williamsburg, walked through the fort announcing the closure of the gates. I suppose the sound of the cannon, which could be heard from miles away, could be used by parents to tell their children that it was time to go to bed but I couldn't find much more to recommend it.

***

Breakfast the next day was much of the same. Actually, it was exactly the same minus the champagne, which I supposed was only available the day before because it had been Christmas morning. Natalie would tell us many times during the week, "The guidebook says meals will be repetitive". And repetitive they were.

I wasn't the only one complaining about the food options. Others in the group grew tired of hearing, "chicken or pork?". I would have thought more fish would be available, being an island, but in researching this when I got home it seemed like most of the fishing boats were so old and couldn't be used, as they could not afford the materials necessary for the maintenance.

Just after breakfast I mailed myself a postcard. The hotel said there was a postal system between Cuba and the US and I wanted to see how long it would take to arrive, if ever. (It did finally arrive about 30 days after I returned home.)

Since I was up early, I also had time before meeting the group to walk around the town a little. I really wanted to get a photo of the banner that hung across one of the streets that said, "Socialismo o Muerte". That coupled with the old cars was just too good of a photo opportunity to pass up. Getting outside and walking around the town without the group also allowed me the time to really see the city.

People were out getting their morning coffee; neighbors were hanging out on their porch steps chatting with one another. Besides all of the people, it was a great chance to get up close to the homes and admire the architecture.

There was one home in particular on a corner that captured my eye. It was a two story Victorian, old and rundown and yet so beautiful. The house itself had lovely architectural details and the garden was well maintained. There were also several cats hanging out, including one kitten, running around chasing butterflies and lapping up water which had pooled in the driveway.

Our first "people to people" activity of the day was a meeting with a representative from the Instituto Cubano de Amistad con los Pueblos (the Cuban Institute of Friendship). Yamil talked with us about Cuba's history, politics and a major focus of the conversation was on the "Cuban 5".

None of us on the tour knew who the Cuban 5 were before arriving in Cuba and to be honest, we probably don't really understand the situation any more now that we have more information. From what we were told, the Cuban 5 are five men being held in US prisons for espionage against the US. Cuba's side of the story is different, saying they were in the US to try to learn about planned attacks against Cuba by US citizens in the 1990's. Throughout Cuba, you will see large billboards and other propaganda of the five men, requesting their return.

I asked a lot of questions during the ninety minutes we were all together but Yamil was happy to respond as best he could. I wasn't ever really sure if I was getting a canned government sanctioned response or a true opinion from him but I was pleased he was at least trying to answer my questions. And it seemed he enjoyed our conversation so much that he decided to join us on our tours the next day. Or perhaps, based on my questions, he was concerned that I might start a revolution.

After leaving the Cuban Institute of Friendship, we drove to Cayo Hueso to visit a community project called "La Casa del Niño y la Niña". Here we met with teachers and students who were involved in a community based project to help them with their schooling as well as art and cultural studies. This part of Havana was very run down and one thing I noticed immediately was that there were no trees, shrubs or flowers anywhere except for the small planters some people had hanging off their balconies. It was a concrete jungle.

We were grateful to meet the kids and teachers, especially since they were all out of school for the holiday week and could have been outside playing with their friends rather than hanging out with us. The room was very small, compared to community centers in the US, and each wall was painted a different color. It had many educational toys, books and musical instruments as well as a computer and television set, though the latter two looked like they were at least fifteen years old.

While the Director of the project did much of the talking in the beginning, many of the kids also had a chance to speak about the project's impact on their life. They were all intelligent, well-spoken and full of ideas and hope.

The motto of the project is: Listening to young voices and taking them into account for a better world. From what I gathered from the meeting, children, in Cuban society, are highly valued. They are all aware of, and even recited for us, the basic principles of the United Nations Convention on the Rights of the Child, Article 31. They even have a song about it which they sang to us.

When I asked them what they wanted to be when they grew up, they all had a different answer: a singer, baseball player, teacher, actor, physician, artist, musician. Depending on their talents, anything was possible. After all, education in Cuba is free. Even for more advanced degrees like law, medicine and PhD programs. If you have the grades, you can become whatever you want. You can even receive multiple degrees and be a perpetual student. Now that doesn't mean you'll actually make any money in Cuba...

On the way to La Mina Restaurant for lunch, we convinced Margarita to take us to the beach in the afternoon. None of us really wanted to do the afternoon activity which was just to walk around Old Havana again and purchase souvenirs. We had to pay extra for their time and gas but we all agreed it would be worth it. It was only the second full day there but we all wanted a little time to relax, get out of the city and not have a scheduled activity.

I have to admit the meal at La Mina was actually decent – not great, but decent. I had roasted vegetables, beans and rice. While we were in a city area which was mostly made up of concrete and buildings, we all noticed that there was a chicken wandering around the patio area of the restaurant. Maybe it had figured out its fate and was trying to break free from wherever it had come.

The highlight of the afternoon was definitely going to the beach. Without a doubt, it was probably one of the best activities of the week. There was a band playing music, the sun was hot overhead, with a slight breeze coming off the Caribbean Sea and the water was a gorgeous blue green. As it swept over my feet, it was pleasingly warm and crystal clear against the pristine white sand.

The beach we were at, Playa Santa Maria, was located about twenty miles east of Havana. It was very crowded that day; being a holiday week. It seemed many tourists and locals had ventured there like us, to take a break from city life and enjoy the tropical warmth, albeit the start of winter.

We managed to get eight lounge chairs all in one central location and a few of us went to the bar for cold beers. Many of the lounge chairs were broken, but they seemed to still work. During the trip, Sara coined the phrase, "That's Cuba for ya" and this was just another great example.

Everything was a little disheveled but you made it work; after all, you

really had no choice.

Dinner that night was at El Aljibe and again, it was a little odd and thrown together, especially my vegetarian meal. I had an omelet, beans and rice with a side of vegetables and French fries. I think the fries are what really threw me. It was one of the better restaurants we visited that week, boasting more locals than tourists which I always find promising. The rest of the group said the chicken was good. Margarita had told us that El Aljibe was known for its chicken, which was cooked in a very special secret sauce.

While we were there, Mike ran into a man he used to work with at Goldman Sachs who was traveling with his daughter. We all laughed and made comments about it being a small world. He worked for a nonprofit organization that I greatly looked up to and admired.

Though I didn't want to be so gauche as to pass him a copy of my resume while he was traveling, I fantasized about the opportunity to be one of their staff photographers, especially in the Central America division. A girl can dream, right? Sara also ended up running into her current boss during the trip. Really, it was the most amazing coincidence that we all ended up on that little island together.

***

Our last full day in Havana we first went to the Literacy Museum where we learned Cuba has had a 100% literacy rate since 1961. I was a little skeptical of that statistic but as the Director of the program talked, I came around and started to believe that it might actually be possible. Education is extremely important in Cuba.

While we were waiting for the shuttle to pick us up, we watched a group of kids playing baseball in a park across the street. Margarita still hadn't confirmed if we'd be going to a baseball game so I figured I might as well enjoy this now as it may be my only opportunity. The game wasn't on the itinerary for the week but I had made the request the first day and Margarita had said she'd look into it.

I wasn't really sure if she liked me that much, given the difficulty I was causing with my eating habits, so I began to ask others in the group to mention their desire to go to a game as well.

No matter where you go, if the demand for something is high, then the supply will often be satisfied.

We then visited Coloreando Mi Barrio, another community based art project. The kids who participated in the project weren't there as it was still the holiday week but we were able to see the artwork and hear from the Director of the program. He mentioned that a famous Hollywood actor would be coming by later that afternoon; it was someone who made an annual trip to Cuba and each time he brought supplies for the kids. We all wondered who it could be but the Director wouldn't tell us.

Driving through the streets of Havana before lunch, Margarita told us we were in an area called Miramar. This was a part of the city that had a more affluent feel to it. The homes were well maintained, large and with acreage. The streets were wider and sidewalks were lined with trees and grass. The center medians were large and park-like with benches spread out every few feet. I didn't really understand this area of Havana because, in socialism, there isn't supposed to be "haves and have-nots". Without a doubt, there was a discrepancy between this part of Havana and other parts we had been to like Cayo Hueso.

This brought me to my question of what exactly is Communism? The way it was told to me by Cubans who I met and spoke with was that communism was similar to the Buddhist's view of enlightenment. It was a lifestyle they were striving for but hadn't yet been able to reach. According to them, not even the USSR had ever reached a true communist society. While I had read the Communist Manifesto in grad school, I didn't remember it ever being discussed in a way that sounded like attaining enlightenment, so I found that idea really intriguing.

In researching communism, I became more captivated because much of it was so closely related to what was happening in the States with the "Occupy Movement" and the 99%. I found this quote about it:

"In it (The Communist Manifesto) they declare that many problems in society are due to the unequal distribution of wealth. To bring about happiness and prosperity for all, the distinctions between the rich and poor of society must be eliminated. And since the rich will never give up their goods or status voluntarily, a rebellion of the poor -- the working class -- is necessary." (source: allaboutphilosophy.org)

It sounded awfully familiar to me... while the Occupy groups hadn't reached the stage of violence, they were highlighting a disparity between the classes. Many have said that soon we will no longer have a middle class in the US; it will be the poor and the rich, the haves and the have-nots.

Communism (I think) is a concept that attempts to provide equality to all. Although it didn't quite succeed in practice, with the definite gap between those with wealth in Cuba and those without, I suppose that was why the people I spoke with acknowledged that Cuba hadn't yet reached a true communist state. I wondered what it would take and why, after fifty-four years they not been able to succeed.

***

Our driver dropped us off at a local outdoor market and we had an opportunity to walk through it and see the items for sale. Mostly, it was local farmers with fresh produce and eggs but there was also one table for toiletries, a flower stand and a small meat section. However the prices for these products were so high (by Cuban standards) that it was very difficult for the average Cuban to purchase them. And because of this, next to the outdoor market was a large warehouse for the food that was rationed.

Before coming to Cuba, I didn't really know much of anything about their "Special Period". Cuba and the Soviet Union really weren't on my radar in the 1990's. I was sixteen when the Cold War ended and really had no knowledge of what the Cold War was because my history lessons in school only dealt with history leading up to the 1929 recession. I didn't really pay attention to the news as a teenager. I quickly got up to speed upon arriving in Cuba about what the Cold War ending meant for them.

They were totally cut off from any resources such as food, medicines, oil, building, and other supplies they would have normally received from the USSR. During the Special Period, food was purchased on a daily basis because they would have electrical outages that could last up to 18-20 hours a day, spoiling any food in their refrigerators (for me, that would make vegetarianism an obvious choice since meat goes bad but veggies do not!). Things considered basic necessities in the States, such as toilet paper, were scarce and/or expensive.

Not growing up during the start of the Cold War and the 1961 missile crisis, it was so insane to me to think that the US has continued its embargo against the Cubans all these years. Considering we are only ninety miles from their shore at the shortest point, we could have easily and cheaply provided them with the necessary products to help them.

I know there are always two sides to every story and honestly, I wasn't really clearly camped out on either side. We were told that on an annual basis, Fidel Castro had asked to speak with the US government in order to try to remedy the embargo/blockade. Fidel insisted he be seen as an equal and respected for his country's ideals (of socialism) and each time, the US had refused to meet with him.

Considering China is a communist country and the US is definitely in bed with them, I was certain there had to be more to that story, if it was even true. It could just be something the Cuban government tells its citizens to maintain a high level of dissatisfaction with the United States.

I was also told that many kids who were born during the Special Period have had a hard time adjusting to life since then. It seems like, during the 80's, the Cubans had a bit of a "heyday" (for lack of a better term considering they still weren't considered a "free" country) and they tried to tell the kids of the 90's that someday, life would return to what it was like back then.

I thought it was doubtful. Unless the US lifts its embargo, Cuba will probably never get out of its precarious situation. Even if the embargo was lifted, I wasn't sure Cuba had the infrastructure to handle the number of tourists who could decide to visit. It was suggested that billions of dollars had been lost in the last fifty years because of the US banning travel to Cuba. Now that, I believed.

As an island under US embargo, Cuba's food resources were extremely limited. It was mentioned to us that any container ship which entered Cuba's ports was not allowed to enter any US port for six months after. That, too, seemed unbelievable but upon returning home, I learned it was indeed true.

While the ships did still sometimes bring in food and supplies, the shipping companies levied heavy additional fees on Cuba in order to offset the loss they were taking by not being allowed into US ports. In 2012, the US government was proposing a similar ban on the countries of Iran, Syria and North Korea. I was really surprised that such a ban had existed in Cuba since 1992 but hadn't yet become a policy in other, much more volatile nations. I couldn't help but wonder if the US was really that worried about Cuba invading...

In my research, I found a shipping company statement claiming to export certain goods to Cuba from the US every other week. The items they could bring in were agricultural and forestry related: live animals, slaughtered animals, milk, eggs, cheese, most other types of food like vegetables, fruit and grains. Wood products were also on the list.

However, just because these items were allowed didn't mean that the Cuban people could afford them. It did explain the "Old Virginia Apples" container boxes we saw one day while walking around Havana. Our driver, Fernando, told me one day that his favorite fruit were apples from California.

All of this information helped lend perspective to the food rationing I heard about and experienced while traveling in Cuba. They didn't have enough food to feed everyone so they rationed essential items like rice, beans, eggs, meat and milk. Of course, I didn't consider the last three items essential, but I digress.

Every Cuban was given a ration book at the beginning of the year and each time they went to the market, they handed the book to the clerk and were given certain items at a subsidized rate. If they needed more than what was allocated to them, they had to pay a higher rate, which I was told was normally the case as the rationed amount was not enough.

It was still cheaper than what we would pay for the same things in the States but I couldn't imagine enjoying having my food rationed or not having an abundance or variety of foods to choose from. I questioned why vegetables weren't included with the rationing and made available to more people.

I imagined the weather conditions in Cuba were ideal for growing them and that it would take far less space and energy to grow vegetables than it did to raise animals for slaughter. In addition to the cost benefits, I found it odd to overlook the additional health bonuses as well.

While we had all paid a pretty steep price for the trip, it was definitely not reflected in our meal options (or our accommodations, for that matter). I think everyone in the group would agree that our perspective had really been broadened as to what rationing meant for the Cuban people.

The lack of variety and even the smaller portion sizes we received at most meals really made us think about the food we ate at home and feel gratitude for the abundance of options in the US and other, more developed countries.

***

After the visit to the market, we walked down to the Friendship House for lunch which was uneventful other than the fact that yet another restaurant informed me that they didn't have beans.

Truly, Cuban vegetarians must be the most disciplined and devoted people anywhere to maintain their eating choices under such conditions.

Our next stop was the Revolution Museum in Old Havana, which used to be the Presidential Palace. I realized this was my in to asking where the President (now Raul Castro) lived currently. Yamil told me that people in Cuba did not know where the Castro families lived. They believed it was somewhere in Havana but did not know exactly where. That seemed so odd to me... considering 1600 Pennsylvania Avenue is one of the most well-known addresses in the US, possibly the world.

Even if there were rebels and they killed the leader, there was assuredly someone below him that would assume power. I supposed since it was Fidel who led the Revolution against Batista, taking over the country in 1959, it only made sense that he would want to hide from people in order to protect himself from a similar fate.

I wasn't really interested in the museum so instead I spent the next two hours talking with Yamil, asking him all kinds of random questions. He seemed to enjoy it though and it was a much more informative exchange for me than what I would have learned from the museum.

One of my first questions was about how Raul Castro came into power. I had seen the following quote while researching Cuba and also remembered hearing news reports about the event when it happened.

"Castro handed power to his brother last week to undergo emergency intestinal surgery. His health remains uncertain, fueling rampant speculation about his legacy." (Source: National Geographic)

That was how the news, in the States, reported Raul Castro taking office - that Fidel had handed the position to his brother when he became ill. In response to my question, Yamil paused before responding and smiled at me; looking back he was probably laughing a little on the inside. He probably thought I was unbelievably naive.

He told me that Fidel most certainly did not hand the country over to his brother when he stepped down but instead the government chose Raul to be his successor because of his long-term commitment to Cuba and because he maintained the same ideals as his brother and the government. He seemed to believe that the inaccuracy was misrepresented on purpose to further propaganda.

Of course, Cuba got US politics and actions wrong too. One of the participants on the tour had picked up a book that talked about the Haiti earthquake and stated that, "The US sent their military into Haiti to take over." It wasn't mentioned that the military was sent because they were trained to help in disaster relief. It was clearly designed to paint the US as the country that took over other countries, particularly as it omitted information about the millions of dollars the US government, private organizations and people donated to the Haitians.

While we did talk quite a lot about politics, I was more interested in his personal life and life in general, in Cuba. Yamil was about my age and told me he was married and had been for ten years. He had one child, a boy, and hoped to have a girl once his wife finished her PhD program. She was studying geography. They lived in a small apartment and were fortunate as they could afford to live by themselves, without extended family.

He mentioned that in the past, Cubans would often have many kids (sometimes eleven or twelve.) but now because of scarce resources, they knew they could not support as many children and the average family now only had one or two kids.

Because of his job with the Friendship Institute, Yamil had been able to travel to other Caribbean countries and Jamaica was his favorite place to visit. He also had dreams of visiting the United States, Egypt, and France. Most people couldn't travel out of the country, not so much because they weren't allowed as it was an expense they couldn't afford.

The minimum monthly wage a person makes in Cuba is $10 US and the average seems to be about $20 (which is $240/year). A few other statistics really caused me to think: about 1% had a cell phone, 2% had access to the internet and less than 10% had a home phone. The last number really sat with me because while many people in the US no longer maintained a home phone, it was only because each individual in the home had a cell phone.

The 2% that did have access to the internet usually had it because of either work or school. Many websites were also restricted and the Cuban people believed the government was monitoring which websites they visited. There were a few internet cafés in the cities but while it was only a few dollars for an hour or two of usage, the cost is beyond what most Cuban people can afford to spend.

Wages in Cuba were paid by the government. This was another challenging notion to get my head wrapped around. With the exception of a few farms and paladares (that the government recently allowed people to own), everyone worked for the government. The government owned all the businesses.

Part of me felt like, in some ways, that may have been a positive, as it would mean everyone would have a job. In other ways though, I felt like it restricted freedom of being able to do what you wanted and pursue your dreams.

The assumption by many people in the US is that Cubans are not free and are under lock and key from the communist government and certain realities there led me to see where this point of view had come from.

I asked Yamil if he felt like he was free and he said he did. I couldn't help but feel like his perception of freedom was limited. He didn't know what it was like to have freedom of the press, as there were only five television channels in Cuba and all television, radio and printed media are either run or monitored by the government.

He also didn't know what it was like to have individual rights, like owning property or a business. If he were to go to the US without permission, he would be banned from ever returning to Cuba. That was a long way off from fitting my definition of freedom, though I had to respect the fact that he was content with what he had in life.

Yamil did say there were times when he wished he could make more money and have a new car or a larger home, but it didn't frustrate him or anger him that he wasn't able to have those things. He was content overall with his life. Material possessions were not important to him compared to all that he had in the way of family, community and his life overall.

Our last activity of the day was a tour of the Rum Museum. While I was excited about this in the beginning, I realized quickly this was not going to be very much fun. There were at least fifty people on the tour and it lasted about twenty minutes. The only good thing about it was the tasting at the end but even then, we only got to taste one 7-year old rum and not any others. It would have been nice to compare other years to understand the differences in taste, but this was Cuba, not Sonoma, and free samples were hard to come by.

Dinner that night was at La Veranda, the same place we had breakfast every morning. I was happy to see a pasta station where they let me select the ingredients for a made-to-order sauce but was not so happy to see the dead pig with an apple in its mouth at the next station over.

Natalie and Nathan showed up late to dinner excited to share with us that they had just seen a famous celebrity in the bar upstairs. Natalie described him wearing a sombrero and seated by himself. I just couldn't imagine this person wearing a sombrero, so Mike and I decided to go searching for him.

We first went to the bar where they had originally seen him but didn't find him there so we walked around the hotel for a while to no avail. We eventually gave up and went back downstairs for dessert.

Chapter 14
Pinar del Rio

"A kiss is a lovely trick designed by nature to stop speech when words become superfluous."
Ingrid Bergman

Since I'd never been a city girl, I was relieved when we finally left Havana and headed west to the province of Pinar del Rio. The drive out there reminded me of the Guanacaste region in Costa Rica. There were hillsides covered in trees, vast landscapes of open space and cow pastures.

Our first stop was in Soroa at a botanical garden known for its orchids. We took a tour while our guide talked about the types of plants in the garden and I felt right at home. Everything reminded me of Costa Rica. Though the palms were a little odd; their trunks were a bright white color.

After the garden tour, we went down the street to walk to a waterfall and then have lunch. Lunch was at the entrance to the waterfall path and as usual, came with cabbage, tomatoes and cucumbers. I also had an omelet, beans and what I think was mashed yucca. I wasn't sure what dessert was. It had a slice of cheese that was brie-like with what was possibly an apricot marmalade, both of which were floating in some type of light orange liquid. While I'm always interested in creating new dishes, this was not something I had any desire to replicate at home.

We then drove to a tobacco farm and learned the process of cigar making.

It was a beautiful piece of land and it was there that I first noticed the

stillness.

There were no cars driving by and everything was very quiet, you could hear the rustling of the tobacco plants in the wind. The property also had a few small farm animals on it which I was sure would be turned into dinner at some point.

In general, people cannot own property in Cuba because of its socialist philosophies. However, Raul Castro had recently allowed some people to own land again and farm it. This was due to the food shortages they were experiencing and the need for more farmers to grow produce and raise livestock for the country's citizens.

A few people purchased cigars and we then headed towards the town and our hotel. Arriving at the hotel though, I had a very bad feeling. The lobby looked like it was from the 1950's and not in the charming throwback sort of way. One of the first things I noticed was the bar was open 24 hours, had loud music playing and our rooms were just above it.

I was talking to Lindsay after we had settled into our unacceptable rooms and she kind of dared me to find out if we were in the right rooms (and at the right hotel). She'd been kidding, but looking at their rate sign in the lobby, it seemed like there was a better room available at a higher rate.

I was pretty sure that, if we were supposed to be at this hotel, then we should have been in the more expensive rooms as we were paying for a 5-star hotel.

I was also curious if they had internet so I took Lindsay's dare and asked the front desk clerk those two questions. I could tell he did not appreciate my questions as answered no to both, in a very disgruntled way. He did elaborate a little by informing me that internet was "at the other hotel".

When I asked where that was he simply said, "Seven blocks," and motioned with his hand toward the front of the lobby. I wasn't sure if he was pointing me in the direction of the other hotel or if he was shooing me away. I was irritated that he insinuated that I should know the name of this other hotel and where it was. He really was not helpful at all.

One of the tour participants (I won't name names) had the idea to just drink a lot and then maybe we wouldn't notice our unacceptable surroundings or the really gross beds and pillows in the rooms.

A few of us found our way to the bar, where once again, they were out of Cristal. I just couldn't understand how all of these places could be out of this one particular beer. A man at the rum museum had informed me that Cristal was for women, Bucanero for men. Could it be there were so many women drinking the Cristal they had run out? Or just that Cristal was a better tasting beer and both men and women were drinking it much more than Bucanero? My money was on the latter.

Either way, the beer they did have was only $1 so I quit complaining and drank up. Of course, after several beers I had to use the restroom and made the mistake of going into the one near the lobby. It was the only one around so I assumed it was co-ed but wondered if maybe there was a women's elsewhere. The stall door didn't close or lock, there was a urinal next to the stall and there was no toilet paper. I thought to myself, "Oh my god, where are we staying?"

As we drank and smoked our cigars, I noticed a man across from us in his baseball uniform, with dirt on his pants from where he must have slid during the game.

As it turned out, that lousy hotel did have one thing going for it...the players from both national baseball teams were staying there that week. I couldn't help but stare at the man, he was really good looking and I did have a bucket list to check off. The fact that I'd had a few bucaneros didn't help matters.

Unfortunately for my list, Daniel, Sara and I then decided to go for a walk around the town at dusk, leaving the cute baseball player behind. We didn't have any particular place to go; we just kind of wandered down the streets and checked out the local community.

A group of older people had set up a table in the road to play dominoes, throwing down the pieces with fervor. Kids were playing soccer in the street, and other people were hanging out talking with one another. There was such a beautiful sense of community. It was really nice to just walk around and see life happening in such a simple and sweet way. Without the need for digital devices.

Given the statistics I mentioned earlier about the cell phones, internet and televisions, it wasn't surprising to see such a strong sense of community amongst the Cuban people. After all, they weren't sitting at home, on the internet, glued to the TV or playing video games. They are outdoors, socializing in person with their neighbors.

It was a refreshing difference from the typical communities in the States where people got home from work, pulled into their garages, closed the door and went inside versus the people in Cuba who set up a card table in the street and play a nightly game of dominoes with their neighbors.

Granted, there were some who might argue that Cuba took their community building a little too far. They had groups called the Committees for the Defense of the Revolution (CDR). From what I could tell, they were like a crazy Homeowner's Association on steroids. I feel qualified to make that assessment because I used to manage community associations and vividly remembered the insanity of it all.

It seemed to work for Cuba, though. Each community had a CDR and each one elected officials to help manage it. They were the watchdogs in the community. They knew everything that was going on, in each household, and they took action when needed. Sometimes it was protective, when someone had a drinking problem, the CDR reps would help the person get to counseling. Or, not that this is wrong or right necessarily, but we were told stories that when people die, sometimes the CDR isn't notified so that the ration books of the deceased could still be used by other family members.

Other times, I would say, it went a little too far. I had no desire for my neighbors to know my personal business. I shared quite a bit about myself in my writing, but that was entirely different. There was no choice involved the CDR.

I think they were, at one time, supposed to monitor the people in the neighborhood in case anyone decided to rebel against the revolution and political regime. Perhaps they still did, which struck me as really repressive. While I would have enjoyed the community connection, I didn't want to trade it for people monitoring my every move. I wouldn't be moving to Cuba any time soon.

***

We returned to the hotel and met the group in the lobby for dinner. I noticed there were even more baseball players hanging out. I couldn't have been happier in that moment; they were all just so cute in their uniforms.

We had to leave for dinner and once again, I had to leave my baseballers (as my friend Lia in Australia calls them) behind.

Margarita told us that even though it was the home team playing, they still had to stay at the hotel as a team, as there were restrictions on what they could do during the season. She told us they had bed checks and curfews and were not allowed to drink or have sex because it would diminish their energy level on game day.

I couldn't stop laughing when I heard that. Not only was that so different from how sports teams handled themselves in the States but I guessed it meant I wasn't going to be hooking up with any baseball players while I was there. I supposed I'd have to visit again during off-season.

In the morning, after a restless night of very little sleep since the music from the bar continued to play past 2:00 a.m., I realized we were not at the originally intended hotel. Our emergency contact sheets the tour company had sent the week prior had listed another hotel as the one we'd be staying at while in Pinar del Rio.

Where we were staying was obviously not the 5-star we were supposed to be at. This seemed a little sneaky and underhanded to me. If we had been told at the start there had been a change, then I wouldn't have been so upset but it was almost as if the tour company was hoping we wouldn't figure it out and could just pocket the extra money.

I ran into Margarita before breakfast and told her about this and she insisted we were at the correct hotel. I then showed her the emergency contact sheet and she reiterated that we were not supposed to be at the other hotel. She confirmed that the current hotel was 2 or 3-stars at most, as opposed to the 5 we'd been expecting. Really, it was 1 star. It was worse than the Motel 6's I stayed at in high school during Spring Break.

The group got together though and I guess you could say we had our own little revolution that morning, complaining about additional issues at the current hotel. Margarita kept insisting the other hotel was full and had no rooms.

This wasn't going over well with anyone in the group, with the exception of maybe Ben who didn't see anything wrong with his room, the awful breakfast with the watery coffee or the hotel in general. Of course, Ben was a college student and a guy; he could have probably slept anywhere and been happy. (no offense to Ben, of course, I'm just relaying my own memories of university.)

As a group, there wasn't much we could do except express our concerns and we decided if we couldn't do anything in that moment, we'd deal with it when we returned to the States.

After breakfast, we drove to Viñales Valley, a UNESCO world heritage site, stopping at the lookout point near Los Jazmines Hotel. Now this looked like a 5-star hotel. We wondered why we weren't staying there. While our scheduled activity of the day was to take a tour of Viñales with a local guide, we had all agreed we would skip that part of the tour, visit the local town and then go to a baseball game in Pinar del Rio.

Viñales was beautiful. It had enormous rock structures that seemed to rise out of nowhere creating massive cliffs, with heights reaching almost one thousand feet, and valleys below which were used for agriculture, using traditional, organic methods. The vast majority of the land had tobacco growing on it.

It was a magnificent view, even more so since out of the hundreds of acres we could see, there was only one very plain home in sight. This was vastly different from other beautiful places in the world which have been overrun by development.

There were also numerous caves to be found in the area but I was glad we didn't go into any, as I was sure my fear of small spaces would have taken over. I also feared there would be bats on the ceilings and I wasn't crazy about the idea of things flying around my head.

When we went for a walk in town, Nathan and Ben went into a tiny market and came out laughing. They were highly amused by the random assortment of items for sale and I had to go inside and see for myself. There were a few bottles of alcohol, a few other miscellaneous items and thousands of eggs. None of us were able to come up with a logical explanation, but we knew we'd never forget that market.

On our way back to the town, Margarita informed us the other hotel ended up having a few rooms available and if we still wanted to, we could switch hotels. We found it interesting that all of a sudden, they had five rooms available when the night before they'd been booked to capacity.

It still seemed shady to me but I just decided to be happy and deal with the issues of the night before when I returned home.

The baseball game started at 10:00 but we arrived just after 11. I didn't mind at all since I didn't really think baseball was a particularly fascinating sport, I just wanted to experience a Cuban baseball game as I had heard Cubans were very passionate about their fandom.

I wasn't disappointed, except for the fact that there was no beer being sold which I thought was really odd. The fans in the stands were all very lively; talking about the game, players and they especially got involved when they felt the umpire had made a bad call or the bases were loaded. I could imagine Cubans being just as lively when they talked about politics.

The Vegueros team of Pinar del Rio, the home team and last year's champions, were playing against the Cienfuego Elefantes. Our seats were right on the third base line and what was really fun to watch were the kids in the stands and how the players would interact with them when the teams changed sides.

As the players walked back to their dugouts from the outfield, the kids in the rows next to us would catch their attention and the players would acknowledge them and reach up to shake their hands. You could see the sparkle in the kids' eyes as they shook the hands of the players. You knew they were hoping to someday be down on that field, playing ball.

Pinar del Rio lost and we returned to our hotel to pack our bags and switch to the better hotel. Margarita told us we should leave our bags at the front desk and go to the restaurant for lunch as we couldn't be late for the next activity.

It always seemed we were running late but it was never the group's fault. Our lunches nearly always took two hours.

That lunch was the first meal of the week where we were given a menu. While I still didn't have many options, I was able to order a cheese pizza. Three beers later (Bucanero, mind you, because this hotel was also out of Cristal), our meals finally arrived. We honestly didn't know what took so long but we were famished and ate quickly, which allowed us to get to our next activity.

Again, it seemed like Cuba's infrastructure just couldn't handle large groups even though there were only eight of us. The tour company actually allowed up to sixteen people in any given tour and we knew we were fortunate to be a small group as we probably never would have been able to go to the beach or the baseball game if there had been more of us.

I'm glad we didn't miss our visit to the community based art project, Con Amor y Esperanza (With Love and Hope), as it was probably the most heartwarming experience of the week. It was set up for kids and adults with Down syndrome and other mental challenges. Not only were the participants there that afternoon but their families were as well.

They showed us how they created the pieces of art, called collagraph art, and Nathan even tried making one of his own. Once they finished their painting, they used a somewhat primitive printing press to transfer the image onto a piece of paper. At the end of their demonstration, many of the kids spoke to us (Margarita translated) and they shared with us how this project had made a difference in their lives. One even said how the project directors were also matchmakers, as each of the young adults in the program had a significant other.

The project had struggled over the last few years due to funding issues. Without any type of marketing, website or fundraising, it couldn't be easy to cover their costs. They did sell the paintings to help fund the project and I purchased one as a gift for my nephew and a piece for myself that was made by the founder, Carrete. When Carrete learned I was from California, he excitedly told me he was having an art exhibit in Livermore, a few hours from where I lived, in early Spring, and invited me to it. Again, just like with the other artist, Ruben, I wasn't sure if I'd still be living in the country but if I was, I promised to try to attend.

What touched me most about the project was not only did these children have a place to go and learn new talents, becoming an integral part of the community, but they were also supported by their families. Each program participant had at least one family member there with them that day to encourage and support them.

**

After returning from such a sweet afternoon, a few of us decided to check emails since our new, and much improved, hotel offered internet service. The guy at the tour company desk seemed to be in charge of the "tourist computer" (meaning the one with the unmonitored internet, or, at least, we thought it was unmonitored). I gave him three CUC's so Nathan, Natalie, Ben and I could share thirty minutes of time.

While I was waiting my turn, Carlos introduced himself to me and struck up a conversation. With only two days left in the trip and having left all of the baseball players at the last hotel, I had pretty much given up on finding a Cuban man.

But Carlos and I ended up talking for what seemed like hours. Once his work day was done, he invited me for a beer in the hotel bar. When he asked me what my favorite beer was, I told him Cristal, but mentioned the hotel had none. He smiled, told me not to worry, and that he'd be back in a few minutes.

Carlos returned a few minutes later with two Cristals in hand. Knowing how little money Cubans made, it did make me a little more appreciative of the kind gesture. We continued talking for another thirty or so minutes before he put his hand on my thigh and leaned in for a kiss. It totally took me by surprise, albeit a welcome one.

We finished up our beers and decided to go to my room for a little privacy. Just like Troy, he worked at the hotel so we had to sneak him into my room. I wondered idly what my deal was with Latin men who worked in hotels but was distracted by Carlos. He was cute and a good kisser. I really needed to fall into his arms and let heartfelt reckless abandon lead me down whatever road it was going to take. I just wanted to be touched and kissed and have one night of passion with a man who wasn't going to leave me, hurt me, lie to me or die.

Unfortunately, I only had thirty minutes before I had to meet my group for dinner, which was supposed to be followed by a CDR event. I fixed myself up for dinner and told Carlos to meet me back at my room at 9:00. I knew that I'd be able to find a way to get out of the "pot luck" communist block party. In this particular instance, I would much rather spend the night with one beautiful man than spend an evening with an entire community.

Of course, dinner service was incredibly slow and to make matters worse, the electricity went out at one point in the kitchen and they were unable to prepare our meals. When dinner finally arrived, my order wasn't thoroughly cooked, so I had to order a separate entrée. It was truly a comedy of errors, especially when dessert finally came and it was five peach slices from a can. I ate one slice and said goodnight to the group, claiming I was tired and wanted a good night of sleep.

Promptly at 9:00 there was a knock at the door and there was Carlos, with two more Cristals in hand. I giggled, let him in and we spent the rest of the night together. I melted into his warm body as we lay next to one another and drifted off to sleep. Carlos was up before sunrise, as he had to try to sneak out of the hotel and get a change of clothes, before returning in a few hours to start his workday. He told me he'd be back to say goodbye before we were scheduled to depart.

I was checking out at the front desk when Carlos returned. He gave me a kiss on the cheek and told me safe travels and to email him when I returned home. I wasn't sure I'd ever see or hear from Carlos again but I was content with our one night together.

After everything I had been through in 2011, I couldn't have asked for a more perfect way to put everything behind me and begin the New Year.
Not only was my bucket list almost complete but the cherry on top was that he used to play baseball.

Chapter 15
Cuba's Green Revolution

"They say that socialism failed because it did not tell the economy the economic cost of socialism and they look at capitalism and say capitalism will probably fail because it does not tell the market the ecological cost of capitalism."
Howard Lyman

This morning's tour and lunch was what I had been waiting for all week; the final item to check off the bucket list. We were going to Las Terrazas in Sierra del Rosario, a UNESCO Biosphere Reserve and Protected Area. The concept of both the biosphere and the creation of Las Terrazas was interesting.

A biosphere (from the UNESCO website) is:
"Each biosphere reserve is intended to fulfill 3 basic functions, which are complementary and mutually reinforcing:
a conservation function - to contribute to the conservation of landscapes, ecosystems, species and genetic variation;
a development function - to foster economic and human development which is socio-culturally and ecologically sustainable;
a logistic function - to provide support for research, monitoring, education and information exchange related to local, national and global issues of conservation and development."

Las Terrazas was a community created in the 1960's. After hundreds of years of deforestation, this area was designated to not only be reforested but to also create a community in which the people cohabited with the land, protecting and preserving the natural resources, living in a sustainable and ecological manner.

It is called Las Terrazas because the homes were all built on terraces, protecting the soil from erosion

212

during the heavy rain season. There are about 1,000 people who now live in the community and we were told there was also an impressive waiting list.

While it is secondary forest (since it's all been replanted), it is a beautiful and peaceful nature reserve. I can see why people wanted to live there; a calm tranquility was observed at every place we visited. As we walked through the quiet community, we came across many people living out their daily life.

While there, we met Lester Campa, an artist who lived at Las Terrazas in a home overlooking the lake. He invited us into his studio and showed us his beautiful, soulful pieces of art which reflected both the politics of his country as well as environmental issues. His art had been displayed around the world in museums and galleries.

My favorite piece of his was a painting consisting of a white trunk of a palm tree with no fronds. The background of the trunk was black except where its shadow cast a white light at the bottom of the canvas. The black background looked stark and dismal against the dead white trunk. In contrast, the shadow area, painted white, had a black trunk. The shadow featured a live palm tree with palm fronds, reflecting the hope of a better tomorrow. If I'd had enough cash, I would have purchased it as it really struck me.

Las Terrazas also boasted a vegetarian restaurant, El Romero, which I couldn't wait to visit. I had already talked with everyone in the group and let Margarita know we had all agreed to go. Of course, she didn't believe me, so she had to reconfirm with everyone.

She just couldn't understand why anyone would want to eat vegetarian. All week, she kept telling me how the chicken or pork was cooked in a special way and how delicious it was, convinced she would make me a meat-eater by the end of the week.

Meanwhile, everyone on the tour was incredibly tired of eating the "specially cooked" chicken and pork. My group was actually pretty relieved when I asked if it would be okay if we tried out the vegetarian restaurant.

There was still some hesitation, for me included, since most of my "vegetarian meals" during the week, as you know, had consisted of cabbage, cucumbers and tomatoes, but we were all in agreement that we should at least try it.

One of the greatest things about the meal was that the group all agreed it was the best food they ate all week.

The meal at El Romero started off with small bowls of lotus ceviche. From the menu, it said it had lemon, turmeric, onion, and other healing aromatic plants. It was described as "very energetic" and below it, it was suggested we take one another by the hands and with closed eyes, make an invocation to give thanks to nature for food, love, health, harmony, solidarity and peace. We weren't actually given menus so we only saw this later on in the meal but found it a lovely suggestion anyway.

The menu also stated their vision:

That the cows, the chicken, the fish, (...), and all our relatives may live. We offer neither cigarettes nor cigars. Please refrain from smoking in our restaurant. Please share your impressions and leave your opinion in our Guestbook.

Now, this was my kind of restaurant and we hadn't even been served any food yet except for the lotus.

Being there, having this sense of peace and tranquility, was how I wanted to live every day...in a beautiful setting with a warm climate, feeling energized and free, benefiting from a healthy body, mind and spirit in my everyday life and having the energy to give back to others through my positive daily actions, whatever they may be.

Next we were served bread with two different types of homemade spreads. The bread was ridiculously good and I'm not just saying that because all week we had been eating bland white toast and butter with our meals. These were bakery quality, freshly made rolls. They only gave us one each but we would have happily eaten many more had they been brought to the table.

We all ordered the mixed fruit smoothie made from organic pineapple, grapefruit and orange juice. It was mauve in color and came in a tall glass with a reusable bamboo straw. Their menus were also printed on recycled paper.

Our first course was a variety of soups that we all shared by passing around the bowls and trying them out. They were beetroot, cold puree of pumpkin and onion, and a soup made with a thick puree of black beans. The entrée was a large platter, offering us several options to choose from. We all took small pieces of each of the items to try out. While we didn't know what any of them were, we weren't disappointed. Dessert was freshly made strawberry ice cream drizzled with honey.

While I'd always had an issue with germs and sharing food, the group was my family at this point and I didn't even think about it until afterwards. Had I thought of it at the time, I wouldn't have done anything differently as this was how meals should be, sharing with each other the colorful dishes placed before us, talking about the different flavors and textures and being excited about food, acknowledging the fresh, healthy and organic meals so beautifully presented to us.

Maybe, for just a moment, my group forgot they were at a vegetarian restaurant with no meat in sight, and yet still savoring every bite. And for me, I felt like I was at home, in the company of beautiful people, eating at one of the many delicious vegetarian restaurants available to me in the Bay area.

We then walked down the road to Café de Maria, a local coffee shop, for an afternoon coffee drink. There were a lot of ironies that we noticed throughout the week but the one that stuck with me the most was happening upon a man on our walk, pushing a wheelbarrow with a large slaughtered pig in it, after our blissful vegetarian meal.

If that hadn't been bad enough, it was also dissected and lying on its back so we could see everything inside. The man had a big smile on his face and was quite proud of his dead pig, showing it off as we all took photos.

Thankfully, since I was more than a little grossed out by the pig, the coffee at Café de Maria made up for it and was some of the best I'd ever drank.

Our guide introduced us to Maria herself, the owner who lived in the apartment above. She was an older woman and had a look of calm simplicity about her. She was watching us from her open shuttered window and I asked if I could take her photo. It was such a beautiful shot that I couldn't resist and she warmly obliged my request.

The café was open from 9 a.m. – 11 p.m. daily and while those hours seemed odd to me (since most people I knew drank coffee earlier in the day), it just reminded me that in other parts of the world, life is at a slower pace and people weren't necessarily

217

rushing out the door at 7 a.m. to sit in traffic for an hour to get to their wretched job by 8.

That had been what I used to do and I'd despised it so much. Working from home, I had so much more personal time to do things. My daily choices were simpler as well, since wardrobe wasn't really an issue, nor packing a lunch.

I chose the Las Terrazas Coffee, which was listed as: "a refreshing cocktail made with milk, coffee, coffee or cacao liquor, chocolate and ice". Other options included American, Creole, Cappuccino, and of course a drink named for the owner, "Café Maria", which consisted of "a delicious liquor made from Pinar del Rio, espresso crowned with foam".

My drink, while included with the tour, was only $2 and all of the drinks were $2 or less. I grinned knowing that same drink at home would have been around $7-10. While they only offered one size that would be small in comparison to US standards, it was more than enough.

At the bottom of the menu, it gave a brief description of the reason why Maria opened this *café:*

"This lonely space, created for the tasting of the "black nectar of gods" keeps the productive and tasting traditions of the area, which began at the beginning of the XX century when Sierra del Rosario mountain range became one of the most important sceneries of Coffee development in Cuba promoted by French immigrants".

This only reinforced my mission of buying local and supporting small business owners. You simply could not have the same type of experience that we had there in a corporately owned coffee store.

I remembered that every positive choice I made, every time I spoke up for my values, it made a difference in the world. I may not have been able to see its immediate results, but I knew in my heart that change was happening.

As everyone was getting ready to leave, waiting in line for the one restroom, Maria invited me into her home. She gestured for me to sit in one of her rocking chairs and while she didn't speak any English, it was a quiet moment I will always remember.

Her home was simple, the television was on and a cultural show was on the air. There was a small simply decorated Christmas tree in the corner of the room and through the sliding doors, with trim that was painted in a bright blue, I could see clothes hanging from the balcony above, drying in the warm breeze. It made me think how tranquil it must be to live in Las Terrazas. And I took back my previous statement...*maybe this was someplace I could potentially live.*

I didn't understand why the other parts of Cuba didn't have the same capability to serve delicious, healthy meals. El Romero was a state-owned restaurant so it had to be under the same regulations as other restaurants that only served cabbage, tomatoes and cucumbers to their vegetarian clientele.

It remained a mystery to me but I was grateful for the opportunity to have spent time in the eco-community of Las Terrazas and to enjoy a good meal that supported life for all beings.

***

On the drive back to Havana, we came across several cows walking on the freeway. Fortunately, for the cows, there were very few cars on the roads in Cuba, which (I'll mention here) were all paved and well maintained.

Even the roads in Las Terrazas and Vinales were paved; a nice change of pace from the bumpy roads I often traveled on in Costa Rica. Not that I was really complaining about the roads there; they served the purpose of keeping development at bay and letting nature take the lead. There being no real money in Cuba, development wasn't really an issue although times are a changing...

I did feel bad for these cows as they looked scared and not sure what to do given the predicament they had gotten themselves into. I also wondered if they were making a mad dash for freedom, knowing what their fate would ultimately be.

This sighting of the cows prompted us to begin a discussion on the rules about farming in Cuba. Margarita told us all cows in Cuba were accounted for and the farmers were not allowed to slaughter their cows without the permission of the government.

Once given permission, the meat had to be allocated to the country as a whole and the farmer was not allowed to take any for himself. Just like everyone else, he had to follow the allowances in the ration book and pay for what he consumed. If a cow became ill, the farmer had to contact a government official and the official would come out to the farm, inspect the animal and determine if it should be killed.

While I had no idea what the penalties would be for failing to complete the process, I could imagine that one wouldn't really want to get caught doing something illegal in a communist country.

When Margarita explained this to us, she made it sound so normal. Like, there wasn't anything strange about not having the choice to eat the food that you were growing or raising. And for Cubans, it was. It's a socialist principle to share with all what you have. The opposite of this would be hoarding, greed and competition...which are capitalist ideals.

At some point in my schooling, I read the Tragedy of the Commons by Garrett Hardin. I imagined Castro must have read it as well. Written in 1968, it was as if Hardin was seeing the future as it pertained to those countries with capitalist beliefs. The premise of Hardin's work was that at one time, all farmers shared a common piece of land and raised their cattle on it. Individual farmers began to realize they could make more money if they raised more cattle and took over more land. Slowly, the "common areas" of the country became overrun with people hoarding as much land as they could and the

221

resources for cattle raising became scarce, leaving less land for the majority of people to make a living from.

I wondered if it was possible to have a balance.

In Cuba, it didn't seem like anyone was starving but if they didn't have the food rationing system and the socialist principles of sharing, I wondered how they would fare. What would happen if the farmer was able to eat his own food, without having to ration it?

While Cuba's transition to green agriculture was mostly in response to the Soviet Union collapse, it may have been one of the best things to come out of the Special Period. Not having access to chemicals, herbicides and pesticides, Cuba was forced to learn how to farm organically. Having little oil to run machinery, much of the work was done by hand and often times, goods were transported by oxen and horse-drawn carts.

In the past they had allowed the rainforest to be cut down in order to plant sugar cane, coffee, tobacco and firewood. It was estimated that when Columbus arrived, Cuba was made up of 90% forests and when Castro took power, there was 10%. With ongoing reforestation efforts, they now had about 25%.

Their water systems were less than adequate and many of their industries had been dumping waste into the waterways. This explained why we were told the water in the hotel was safe for hygiene purposes only. Even that seemed a little sketchy. While I cringed every time I opened one, bottled water was a must on the trip. Even when brushing one's teeth we had to use bottled water.

One thing I recommended to the tour company afterwards was they should purchase large bottles of water (multi-gallon sizes) and have them available for people to refill their reusable water bottles. This would create so much less waste in the long run and may actually save money.

I couldn't see the pollution (like you can on any given day in Los Angeles), however I knew it existed. All I had to do was look at the 50 plus year old cars and buses on the Cuban roads and see the black smoke spewing out of the tailpipe.

Thankfully, since travel to Cuba was kept at a minimum, the natural environment had remained steadily safe. Boats, jet skis and divers weren't overrunning Cuba's coral reefs. The forests had very few people traipsing through them and the ecological necessities like sandy beaches and trees for birds, turtles and other wildlife are remaining intact and less crowded than many other Caribbean islands.

The ecological diversity found in Cuba was one to be explored, protected and respected. Though I knew that would change as the US loosened restrictions on people traveling to Cuba.

Chapter 16
Reflections on Cuba

"Our battered suitcases were piled on the sidewalk again; we had longer ways to go. But no matter, the road is life."
Jack Kerouac

Returning to Hotel Nacional for our final night, we tried to check in to our rooms but the hotel said they weren't ready (surprise, surprise). We decided to go outside, order mojitos and enjoy the last few hours of sunshine before we returned home to our various cold regions in the States.

We then went on a tour of the hotel grounds and learned about its history. We got to see the rooms where all the famous people had stayed back in the 50's; the mafia, Sinatra, Nat King Cole. We really got the impression that in the glory days, before the Revolution, Hotel Nacional must have been the place to stay at.

The tour guide took us outside and we passed by a cage with little birds in it. They were singing their songs and it was then that I had a moment of clarity.

The Cubans were just like those birds; so colorful, beautiful, full of life, creating beautiful music and art, but locked up in a cage, unable to be free to experience the world. They weren't able to see the world outside their small island nation. Even worse, they didn't have enough money to travel around their own country and see the different provinces.

I, too, could relate to those pretty little trapped birds. While I was free to do most anything I wanted, I would soon be returning home to the misery of being sick every day and trapped inside my house.

Our guide took us into the bunkers which were used during the missile crisis and claustrophobia took over my mental state. We had been warned beforehand but I didn't think it could be all that bad.

It was though; the tunnels were small and old and all I could think was would they hold up if there was an earthquake. We all made it out of them safely though and the fresh air was a welcome sense of relief. One odd thing that occurred while we were in the bunkers was that our guide stopped translating into English when she spoke about the missile crisis. I wasn't paying that close of attention but it was noticed by other people on the tour and we all wondered what she must have said about the US's involvement in the event.

After the tour, we walked up to Coppelia, an ice cream shop Margarita had been telling us about all week. She said Coppelia was the best and most famous ice cream in all of Cuba and we had to try it before we left. I don't know if it's the best I'd ever had but it was good.

There were three flavors to choose from and I chose chocolate mint. The other two were chocolate and vanilla. In the past there were over twenty flavors but with the Special Period, milk became scarce and they couldn't continue to produce them all.

There was more to the story though which I'd only learn later, as it wasn't something Margarita would tell us. There were many times when I wondered if we were getting the full story from her since the government paid her wages and as such, had to be cautious of what she said.

Since Fidel opened Coppelia back in the 60's and had wanted over thirty flavors at that time, I suppose he was trying to offer his citizens a little bit of what the US had with Baskin-Robbins 31 Flavors, which opened in the 1940s.

The Coppelia in Havana was actually a huge park, almost an entire city block it seemed. We asked a security guard where to go for the ice cream and he directed us to an area, away from all of the locals who were standing in a very long line to get their late afternoon treat. I would later learn that we could either wait in the long line and pay a very small amount (a few pennies) or go to the shops where there were no lines and pay with tourist dollars.

Looking back,
it felt terribly unfair;
another example of
have's and have not's.
I would have waited had I
understood better what was
happening.

***

There was a vast amount of culture in Cuba, from art to music to baseball to just the people themselves, it was an amazing opportunity to experience it all. There seemed to be men and women singing and playing musical instruments everywhere we went. I loved walking down the street and seeing people socialize with one another throughout the day.

At night, the Malecón was the major hangout spot for people of all ages in Havana. The smell of cigar smoke permeated the air, inside and out. There were no laws prohibiting smoking in public spaces and I gained so much appreciation for smoking prohibition in California's bars, restaurants and other public spaces.

I loved hearing their music, meeting artists, talking to them about their work and talking with random people to learn who they were and what their life was like. And while Cuban rum and cigars were considered contraband and couldn't be brought into the States, I got the chance to partake in both.

I also decided there must be a gigantic farm of mint growing somewhere in the country considering how many mojitos were being drunk by tourists and locals alike. It was a good thing mint grows like a weed.

I did have one cigar I was taking home with me. Ruben had given it to me and I had thrown it into my luggage. After a week of traveling, I wasn't even sure where it was in my disheveled suitcase and I figured if I couldn't find it, then most likely the customs agents wouldn't either.

It did however make me a little nervous, especially as I approached the immigrations officer and he questioned me, *"Why did you want to go to Cuba? I don't understand why anyone, without family there, would want to visit that country"*.

It was a rhetorical question and even if I had tried to answer him, based on how he asked the question, he still wouldn't have understood my reasoning.

Getting through customs, on the other hand, was a breeze. The only question the Latino agent (who was possibly Cuban himself) asked was if I enjoyed my time in Cuba which I happily responded with, "It was awesome". He smiled at me and let me pass, not questioning anything I had written on the form or asking to see inside my luggage.

I had said my goodbyes to the group while in the immigration line. I knew we'd all be separated at that point and going our separate ways. I really couldn't have asked for a better group of people to be on the trip with.

The entire week, everyone got along; there were never any conflicts or discord. And I really felt like I made some good friends. They were all so kind in inviting me to come visit them on the East Coast and while I probably wouldn't be able to do that before moving to Costa Rica, their offer was appreciated. I did hope I'd be able to see them again someday.

***

As I sat in the Admiral's Club waiting for my flight home, I began to digest all that I had learned and experienced in the past seven days. There were still things I was trying to figure out, though my group would probably tell you that I asked more questions than all of them combined.

While I wasn't certain if there was anything to the belief in past lives, if there was, I'd say that I was probably a socialist in a former life.

The one thing I did know? I absolutely loved the socialist aspects of my life that I already engaged in. While my family is loving and giving to a certain extent, from a very young age, I was taught to be independent and not rely on anyone else.

However I'd chosen a different path. I loved sharing with others and working towards the common good.

In my life, I was proud to be able to say that I'd rejected the philosophy of independence to some extent and embraced the concept that we were all one. When someone asked for my help, I gave it unconditionally. Even if I knew they couldn't pay me for my time or expertise.

In doing this, I've been fortunate to see how my services have helped make the world a better, more loving kind place. I knew I'd made a difference because those who I'd helped had told me how they took what they learned from me and paid it forward, helping someone else.

Money does not make the world go round. Love and sharing do.

That was why I created my business, for Harmony; to connect, communicate and collaborate with others. When I did those three things in a lovingkind way, I created positive ripples in my own life, my community and my world.

I might not make millions of dollars from it and I may never know how many ripples were created and how many lives were positively changed by my actions but I do know that through sharing my talents and experience with others, transformation takes place.

Another thought I had were about my feelings on the absence of freedom in Cuba. It prompted me to dwell on whether or not I was just another caged bird, in a brighter shinier cage.

Sure, I had the freedom to own property and a business, the right to free speech and access the entire random buffet of the internet but how much did my voice really count in terms of what was decided in Washington.

In the democracy the US was so proud of, were my representatives really listening to the people or just playing political games and taking special interest money while presenting the facade of freedom?

For all that our nation claimed to value equality, I'd certainly been in positions to witness inequality. In some of our urban and rural areas families were hungry, some were homeless and schools didn't always have books for the children. Gangs and drugs were rampant. I wondered just how free kids felt growing up in the inner city. Was the US really better off for our capitalist offering of The American Dream?

***

Returning home, I created a new gratitude list::

Clean water from my tap for drinking as well as clean water for my shower, plants and washer

Toilet seat covers in public restrooms, toilet paper and toilet seats

My surrogate family on the trip: Sarah, Daniel, Lindsay, Mike, Ben, Nathan and Natalie

High speed, unrestricted, unmonitored internet along with wifi, both in my house and businesses like my local coffee shop

An abundance and variety of food, drinks and locally owned businesses

While I don't watch much TV, I'm appreciative that I have many choices for channels and programming

I mentioned this one in my last list but the ability to travel and meet new people

The US constitution's first amendment: The right to free speech, religion and to peaceably assemble

Chapter 17
The Journey Home

"Today is your day, your mountain is waiting. So get on your way."
Dr. Seuss

Returning to California, my writers block was miraculously gone. I don't know if it was the night spent with Carlos or the vibrant beauty of Cuba that opened my heart and mind again but the words were finally pouring onto the paper.

I spent hours upon hours writing and typing, not even realizing when the sun had gone down and I was sitting in the dark with only the light from my laptop screen illuminating the room.

A few days after returning, one of the local Mavericks surfers announced on Facebook that he was chartering a boat for the incoming swell and invited interested parties to join him. Though big wave surfing was decidedly different than what I had experienced during my surfing lesson with Oscar, I was starting to really feel like my adventurous, up for anything self again.

Three days later, I was out on that boat, heading out of Pillar Point Harbor towards those beautiful giant monsters that only Mother Nature could create and I was ecstatic. It was one last adventure before I had to buckle down and focus on the planning, packing, sorting and saving for my upcoming move.

My improved mental clarity also made it easier to assess what needed to be done for Harmony. When I returned home he was really sick for the first few days. I began the process of accepting the fact that it was probably time to let go.

It was impossible to think about him not joining me on my next journey in life. He'd been my companion for seventeen years. I adopted him from a pound in 1995 (they were still called pounds back then) and he was just this adorable all black kitten; three weeks old with bright blue eyes which would eventually change to a brilliant yellow-green.

Even though he was a boy, he was named Harmony because he always followed his older sister, Melody, around trying to do everything she did, often unsuccessfully but always making a determined effort. Like the harmony follows the melody, it just fit.

I felt so helpless during this time. I would have done anything to help him, as he was my sweet little boy, but there was nothing I could do. The next few months would be a rollercoaster for me as there were days when he seemed so normal, racing me up the stairs to where he ate dinner or playing with his toys, dragging his stuffed animals around the house.

I'd begin to hope that perhaps he would be able to come with me, but then the next day he would struggle with trying to sit next to me or he wouldn't eat very much and it would remind me that he was not well. I couldn't see blatant evidence of suffering but I guess, in my heart, I knew not being able to purr must have been difficult. I just wasn't sure that was a significant enough reason to opt for euthanizing him.

I resolved to make him as comfortable as possible for the next few months. Perhaps I just hoped to forestall the inevitable but I thought of the days of sunshine he could still experience, the kitty treats he loved and the moments in my lap.

I would often try to brush him, as this was always something he had liked in the past, but it only made him want to purr so even these little moments of joy were challenging.

I needed to let him go and I needed to find the strength to do that. It was just so hard to cope with this decision when he didn't appear ill 99% of the time. I decided to make my decision by the end of March, because he would need a rabies vaccination at least thirty days before the move.

I felt a slight reprieve and bit of peace at that decision, giving the two of us just a little more time before I made any irreversible decisions.

***

Ninety-six days before my move, I purchased my one-way plane ticket to Costa Rica with a sense of delight (to put it mildly). I honestly didn't know if I was more excited about the fact that I would be moving or that I'd be turning in my resignation in seventy-six days. I was ecstatic about both. My elation was so strong that I actually wrote my resignation letter and post-dated it just so it would be ready to go when the day finally arrived.

I was pretty much checked out of my job at this point, just going through the motions. I was trying to stay as far below the radar as I could and just do my work. I wasn't holding my breath they'd keep me on and I had to admit I was a little relieved at the thought of not having to work so much anymore, leaving this part of my life behind and being able to solely focus on my new life on the Rich Coast.

The little extra cash I might receive if they kept me on was an incentive to not completely burn my bridges though, so I kept my head down at work and started to wait it out.

Outside of work, with only three months to get everything together, I was constantly asking myself questions: What was I selling? What could I take with me and what could I have others hold onto? My dear friend in Oregon, Amy, who has six people in her family and only a small three-bedroom house had said she'd hold onto the items I couldn't move with but didn't want to part with just yet. My best friend, Mike, had also agreed to provide storage.

Over the next ten weeks, I spent a little time each day sorting through all the stuff I'd collected over the last seventeen years of living on my own plus everything that I still held onto from my childhood.

Sadly, I'd been simplifying and de-cluttering for years and I still had so much stuff to deal with before moving.

I also had to figure out what I needed to purchase before I left the country. I knew trying to buy new things in Costa Rica would be difficult and expensive. I started a list of what I'd need...definitely new Teva's to replace those that were lost in Panama, a new waterproof camera for the one I lost in the river, an iPad would be nice so I could download books to read rather than having paper copies.

I didn't really need new clothes but I did need to figure out which, if any, of my cold weather clothes were still needed. I knew that I wanted to hike

Chirripo, which would require warmer clothes as it could get down to almost freezing at the summit, so there were valid rationalizations to hold on to some, but other than that, almost all of my business attire could be given to Goodwill and I would try to sell everything else.

I was also making lists of things I needed to do: get my car smog checked and registered before I sold it, renew my driver's license as it was set to expire in November, contact utility companies about shut-off dates, decide what to do about my bank accounts here, file my 2011 taxes (and hope for a good refund) arrange shuttle transportation for when I arrived...so much to do, so little time.

About sixty days before the move, I learned I would need surgery. Just one more thing I needed to do before I left and hope all went well with the recovery as there wouldn't be much time between the surgery and my move date. I was also disappointed that it would wipe out the emergency medical fund I had been saving for the last year.

While the surgery was an unexpected downturn, I experienced elation as Harmony seemed to make a miraculous recovery. Not only could he purr again but he would sit with me and want to be brushed and pet. I decided to get him a pet reservation with the airline so he could come with me in the cabin and because I didn't have to pay for it until arrival, there was still time to determine if he was truly healthy enough to go.

***

Some of the days were spent daydreaming about what was to come.

I knew living in Costa Rica would be different from just traveling there for a few weeks every year, but I couldn't wait for the day when I could finally breathe easily every single day, without the impending return to California.

Just the thought of living in a beautiful environment that nourished my body, mind and spirit was enough to make me want to burst into song and dance about my house. Which, I'll admit, I did at times, twirling on my hardwood floors with Harmony in my arms.

As the weeks went by, I met with friends to say my "hasta luego's", sure it wasn't goodbye as much as a temporary time lapse until they'd come for a visit. While I still had a kitchen table to eat at, I had Chas and his girlfriend, Stephanie, over for dinner. It was a fun evening filled with good conversation, good food and lots of laughter. They brought me a bon voyage gift of a gemstone called tourmaline. It was a small piece of the crystal, the perfect size to hold in my hand and close my fist around and the perfect size to travel with.

What I liked most about its physical properties was that it wasn't a perfectly cut stone. It had ridges and rough edges, reminding me things in life need not be perfect; they could be a little worn around the edges and still be beautiful. They explained to me two of the stone's properties were strength and protection - both of which I needed, making the gift so touching in its significance.

The next day, I did a little googling to learn more about the stone's properties. It was correlated to the root chakra prompting the thought, *"Oh thank god, maybe it will heal my broken tailbone."*

It was said to work as a grounding force, which would hopefully also help improve my overall coordination, protecting me from any future falls considering I'd no longer have health insurance.

Its purpose was to help the body return to homeostasis, especially supporting the endocrine, immune and autonomic nervous systems; all of which had been out of sync for me the last few years.

Last but not least, it helped improve self-confidence and lessened fear. Though I clearly couldn't take every belonging I'd ever loved to Costa Rica, this new treasure would definitely be making the short list along with my baby book, my grandma's wedding ring, a book my nephew gave me a few Christmases before, along with a colorful cat sculpture my dad had given me. Just about everything else I was keeping would go into storage at friends homes, at least temporarily.

While I understood the logical reasons for storing things that were too expensive to ship, I strangely struggled with selling certain items. Like the glassware I'd had since I first moved into my own place seventeen years before and my bedroom dresser and nightstand set made from a tropical salvaged wood, which was the first real piece of furniture I'd purchased as an adult. I found it difficult to really let these material objects go. But I knew I had no choice and I knew they went to good homes.

Another odd part of the preparation process was dealing with the crazy people replying to my Craig's List postings. They seemed to want everything for free, or they'd make appointments with me to pick up the items and not show up. I even had someone show up and hand me several rolls of quarters to pay for the items they were purchasing. I was never a garage sale type so all this was quite bizarre to me.

Not having the money from my parents for this major life event (admittedly still a sore spot despite my renewed gratitude with life after visiting Cuba) was also forcing me to give the house back to the bank.

I needed the cash from not paying for the mortgage to give a boost to my savings. Not the most ideal situation but I have no regrets. As it's been said: *desperate times call for desperate measures.* Or what is often said in Costa Rica: *así es la vida.* Such is life.

I would have loved to have kept it as an investment property and even had a few rental prospects but since my income would be so low in Costa Rica, I wouldn't have the money to pay for any repairs that needed to be done before renting it.

Plus...

Thinking ahead, if a toilet broke or the oven needed repair, there would be no extra money to pay for it. I'd put almost 50K into the house over the last few years but I just had to come to terms with the loss. Besides, at the end of the day, I was going to be living somewhere that I could enjoy good health and that was infinitely more important to me than property.

***

People often asked me why I liked Costa Rica so much.

I loved how vastly different it was from where I'd grown up. The people, the lifestyle and even I was different when I was there. The humidity made my skin glisten and my hair got these soft curls that for the life of me, I couldn't get in the dry air of California.

I had a deep, inexplicable connection to the country that was so difficult to explain to people who were often too caught up in their busy lives in the States. It motivated me to share the beauty of the world, and learn new things about myself. It gave me hope that a brighter future was possible.

The year in between finally deciding to move to Costa Rica and really doing it was filled with so many opportunities to live each day with integrity, truth and compassion. I learned the truth of myself outside of the support of a partner, family and my employer.

I now knew that there wasn't anything that could stand between what I wanted and me.

Fear? I rejected that every time I showed up as my beautiful, uncompromising self, refusing to let anyone else define me or dictate my needs; traveling solo, surfing lessons, questioning communist values and even letting go of the desire to have my family be something they couldn't or wouldn't be for me.

For every time I stuck to my values, whether it was following the yogic path, my vegan tendencies or just believing in myself, my resolve became just a little stronger, clearly giving me the courage and strength to make the move and let go of that which was holding me back.

I felt truly blessed to have the opportunity to work and live in Costa Rica permanently.

Admittedly, this was probably the biggest decision of my entire life, one that I would equate to getting married or adopting a child.

While I didn't know what they were yet, I knew there would be difficulties, adjustments, changes in the days, months and years ahead. But I felt ready.

I had finally reached a place of gratitude for my pain, my lessons, and even my fears. They each played their part in creating the type of woman who could push beyond expectations and Live. Live beyond anything I could have ever hoped or dreamed for...Live in a way that not only supported me, my health, my passion but also live to create meaningful work in the world. And ultimately, to finally feel at Home.

***

Harmony was in his carrier. My suitcases and boxes were packed and in the car. My household furnishings had all been sold. It was time. As Chas, Stephanie and I drove down 101 towards the airport, I remembered that very cold morning a few years before when I asked myself the question, *"Why am I here?"*

At the time, I thought it only had to do with my physical body in cold Northern California but I'd realized that was really meant as a much more existential question and I'd finally answered it. I'd dug deep, past my hurt and fears and finally found myself. I knew who I was; I knew where I was going. I knew what I wanted out of life.

As Harmony and I waited for our flight in the American Airlines Admiral's Club, I felt my body relax. Sipping on a glass of red wine, I eagerly anticipated the first person to ask me where I lived.

I couldn't wait to answer,
"Vivo en Costa Rica!"

My leap didn't have a safety net but I knew there were people who believed in me and supported the choices I was making and many of them were there at my destination, my new home, waiting for me with open arms.

They grounded me, gave me insight and found encouraging ways to help me do better. These were the people who would tell me the following, maybe not in Dr. Seuss fashion, but something along these lines:

"And will you succeed?
Yes. You will, indeed.
(98 and 3/4 percent guaranteed.)
KID, YOU'LL MOVE MOUNTAINS.
So...
be your name Buxbaum or Bixby or Bray
or Mordecai Ali Van Allen O'Shea,
You're off to Great Places.
Today is your day.
Your mountain is waiting.
So...get on your way."

And for that, I will always be grateful. I finally felt ready to begin the next chapter in my life.

To be continued...

About the Author

Chrissy Gruninger's intention for all that she does is to reflect the harmony, the oneness, in all that exists. Through her writing, she shares what she sees and learns, exploring the many facets of the world around us. She lives a meaningful, wildhearted life; one that is in service to others, providing a voice for those who cannot speak up for themselves.

She is a yoga teacher, happiness mentor and received her Graduate Degree in Integrative Health and Sustainability from Sonoma State University in 2008. She is a multi-passionate entrepreneur and owns Social [media] Wellness, an online business management firm and ChrissyGruninger.com.

Chrissy empowers individuals in creating more harmony in their lives and supports professionals in creating more harmony in the world. She offers personalized mentoring based on her signature approach, Inherent Harmony, as well as online business management for wellness and eco companies committed to spreading positive energy.

To further explore ways on how to live A Wildhearted Sanguine Life, one that embodies intentional and mindful action, please connect with Chrissy at www.chrissygruninger.com.

Her Living Well Book Collection and Rich Coast Experiences Collection are available in print or via iBooks and Kindle. These books are designed to teach you to live more intentionally; to experience and become aware of the beauty that is within each of us and all that exists in the world.

Her free 30 day Simply Sanguine Challenge is available at chrissygruninger.com/simply-sanguine-main.

Made in the USA
Las Vegas, NV
01 May 2024